KS3 English

Complete Revision and Practice

Contents

Section One — The Reading Paper

Section Two — Reading Paper: How It's Done

Section Three — Quoting

Section Four — Shakespeare

Section Five — Shakespeare Question: How It's Done

Contents

Published by Coordination Group Publications Ltd.

Editors:
Katherine Reed, Edward Robinson, Jennifer Underwood

Contributors:
Angela Billington, Taissa Csaky, Charley Darbishire, Margaret Giordmaine, Dominic Hall, Gemma Hallam, Sharon Keeley, Simon Little, Alan Rix, Elisabeth Sanderson, Laura Schibrowski, Katherine Stewart, Tim Wakeling, James Paul Wallis, Erika Welham, Nicola Woodfin, Andrew Wright

With thanks to Kate Houghton, Dan Owen, Jennifer Underwood, Jill Webster and Nicola Woodfin for the proofreading.

Acknowledgements

The publisher would like to thank:

J.K. Rowling, *Harry Potter and the Goblet of Fire*, Copyright © J.K. Rowling, 2000
Exodus, *Southern France Classic*, from *Exodus Biking Adventures*, 2003
Greenpeace http://www.greenpeace.org, *Kids for Forests*
Jerome Monahan, *Supermarkets are giving us rubbish*, The Guardian 2002
Livewire (The Women's Press), *The Livewire Guide to Going, Being and Staying Veggie*, Juliet Gellatley, 1996
Penguin Group (Australia), *Spaghetti Pig-Out*, Paul Jennings, from *13 Unpredictable Tales*, 1997
www.eyewitnesstohistory.com, *The Sinking of the Titanic*
Extract from *Cider with Rosie by* Laurie Lee published by Hogarth Press. Used by permission of the Random House Group Limited
University of York, University of York press release, Copyright © University of York
Zlata's Diary: A child's life in Sarajevo by Zlata Filipovic, translated by Christina Pribichevich-Zoric (Viking 1994, first published in France as 'Le Journal de Zlata' by Fixot et editions Robert Laffont 1993) Copyright © Fixot et éditions Robert Laffont, 1993
Stone Cold by Robert Swindells (Hamish Hamilton, 1993) Copyright © Robert Swindells, 1993
Extract from The Listeners by Walter de la Mare. The Literary Trustees of Walter de la Mare and the Society of Authors as their representative.
For One Night Only, from The All Nite Café by Phillip Gross, reprinted by permission of the publishers Faber and Faber Limited.

ISBN: 978 1 84146 384 1
Website: www.cgpbooks.co.uk
Printed by Elanders Hindson Ltd, Newcastle upon Tyne.
Clipart source: CorelDRAW®

Reading Questions

Reading Questions ask you to write about bits of writing you haven't seen before.
They make up a whole paper in your English SATs — so you'd best know how to do them.

*Reading Questions **Aren't** as **Difficult** as you **Think***

You get a few bits of writing to read, and some questions about each one. Don't try to make a big deal about it — you can get good marks by making very simple points.

Three Golden Rules

1) Make simple points in your answers.
2) Get all your answers from the text — don't make things up.
3) Quote to back up your answers whenever you can.

*Read Each **Piece of Writing** Carefully*

Yes, this is a very obvious piece of advice.
It's worth saying though — you don't want to lose a load of marks for something as silly as not reading the questions or the bits of writing properly.

1) Read each bit of writing carefully, so you know what it's about and what happens.

2) Then read through all the questions.

3) After you've read the questions, read through the first bit of writing again with the questions in your mind. Once you know what the questions are, you might spot some things you hadn't seen before.

*It Really is that **Straightforward***

All you have to do after that is answer each question in turn.
The next few pages tell you how to do just that...

Remember the Three Golden Rules

The worst thing that can happen in an exam is thinking that you can't answer the questions. But learn those three golden rules and you'll be ready for anything they throw at you. Make sure you use them for every Reading Question and you'll be fine.

State the Obvious

This is a really important piece of advice. Don't be scared — you don't have to get all complicated to do well in English SATs. You get plenty of marks for stating the obvious.

*You Get **Marks** if you State The **Obvious***

I don't blame you if you read the questions and think "I can't think of anything clever to say." Don't worry — think of something obvious to say. Sensible points will get you marks, even if they hardly seem worth saying at first.

> If you notice something in the text that seems to answer the question, the chances are it does, so write it down.

DON'T think "Oh, that's obvious, there's no point in writing that."
Of course there's a point — the point is you'll get marks for writing it down.

*Here's an Example of Making **Simple Points***

Here's a bit of a story:

> Lee shivered. He pulled his coat tightly around him, although it wasn't cold. His fists were clenched in his pockets. He stared at the floor in front of his feet and occasionally glanced nervously at the other people in the waiting room.

Here's a question:

> Q. What does the writer tell us about Lee's feelings in the dentist's waiting room?

Here goes — the answer.

> *The writer tells us that Lee was nervous and scared. Lee "glanced nervously" at the other people in the waiting room. The writer says he was shivering, "although it wasn't cold". He was staring at the floor, which people often do when they're nervous.*

Here's a bit from the text that's got something to do with the question.

Shivering and scared go together, so mention that he was shivering.

This answer may sound simple, but it's all you need to do to get the marks.

Remember to keep it simple

This is the ultra-important bit of advice for tackling reading questions. Learn it before you go any further. Even dead obvious things are worth saying — they get you marks.

Two Great Tips for Reading

Exams don't have to be complicated. Keep these tips in mind and things will be a lot easier.

Pretend the Examiners **Don't Know Anything**

This sounds bizarre, but it's actually a really good tip. Imagine that you have to explain everything to them because they don't understand anything.

This goes back to the point about stating the obvious. If you don't make the really simple points, the examiner might not know that you have thought about them.

There's nothing worse than making a fabulously clever point and losing out on marks because the examiner doesn't quite understand what you're getting at.

Make sure what you write is easy to understand.

Don't try something like this:

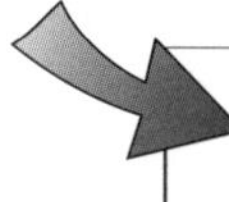

The writer has made Lee a metaphor for the primeval fear which resides in all humankind. The writer identifies his fears with the physical sensation of shivering, giving him a universal, almost Christ-like humanity and calling on our deepest wellsprings of sympathy and self-awareness.

It Doesn't Hurt to **Write Properly**

1) You don't get any marks for handwriting. But if the examiner's just looked at 300 disgustingly untidy answers and yours is the first nice neat one that hits their eyes, they're going to like you.

2) Writing in proper sentences with proper punctuation will make it easier for the examiner to understand the points you're making. Make sure you use the right punctuation for quoting — see Section 3 for how to do it properly.

3) Split your answer into paragraphs, one for each of your main points. It'll make it crystal clear to the examiners that you've made lots of separate points and you deserve lots of marks.

Keep your writing clear and easy to follow

The examiner's first impression of you will be based on how neat your work is. If your writing is tidy and easy to understand, they'll be on your side from the start.

Short Reading Questions

Most of the questions on the Reading Paper are very short ones.

The **Short Questions** Don't Look Too **Bad**

Some of the short questions are really easy. But some of them need you to do a bit of thinking. Read each question a couple of times before you try answering it so you don't mess up.

Some Questions **Check** Your **Understanding**

These questions are testing that you understand what you've read. They're not that hard, so don't make a big deal out of them.

They could ask you to find bits from the writing and write them down.

From paragraph 3, write down how long the Headless Horseman has been living at the inn.

From the fifth paragraph, give three ways in which goblins are different from trolls.

They could ask you to sum up part of the writing.

Most Short Questions Ask You About the **Style**

Most of the short questions ask about the way things are written. Here's an example:

Explain how the first paragraph sets a **gloomy** tone.

The trick with style questions is to look at the detail. Look at each word and decide why it's there.

The hooded man reined in his horse, and wiped the blood from his face. He strained his eyes and ears for a sign that he was nearing safety, but the black night suffocated all sight and sound.

Mention any gloomy words in your answer.

Write about what's happening too. It tells you the man's in trouble and that adds to the gloominess.

Everything you need to answer Reading Questions is there in the texts. Keep reading until you find the answer. Don't make things up.

Don't assume that all short questions are easy

The trick with these short questions is not to get cocky. If you assume they're all easy you could make some nasty mistakes. Read each one through a couple of times and you'll be fine.

Working Out What to Do

Here's what you need to look at on <u>every</u> question to be sure you're doing what they want.

*They **Tell You Where** to Find the Answer*

The question <u>always</u> tells you <u>where</u> to look for the answer.

> Explain how the final paragraph is an effective ending for the story.

Don't waste time going through the <u>whole piece</u> of writing for each question.
Just go <u>straight</u> to the paragraph they tell you to look at.

If the question says "<u>From paragraph 4</u>..." then look at <u>paragraph 4</u>.
The answer <u>will</u> be in there somewhere.

***Give** them What they **Ask** For*

Some questions make life really easy because they <u>tell you</u> what to write.

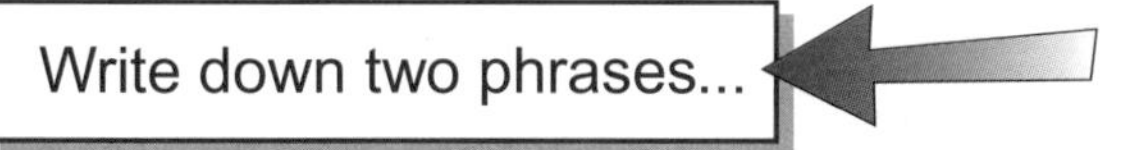

For this you just need to <u>copy</u> two phrases from the piece you've read.

Support your answer with a quotation.

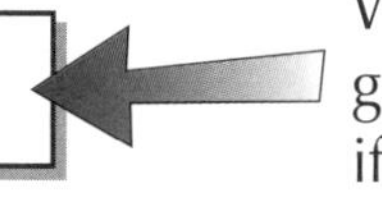

When they say this, be sure to get that <u>quote</u> in your answer — if you forget it you'll lose a mark.

Write down three reasons...

Make sure you give <u>three</u> reasons — not <u>two</u> or <u>four</u>.

***Open-Ended** Questions Are Trickier*

Some questions <u>don't</u> tell you exactly what to say — you have to work it out.

If the question asks <u>how</u>, use <u>by</u> in your answer:

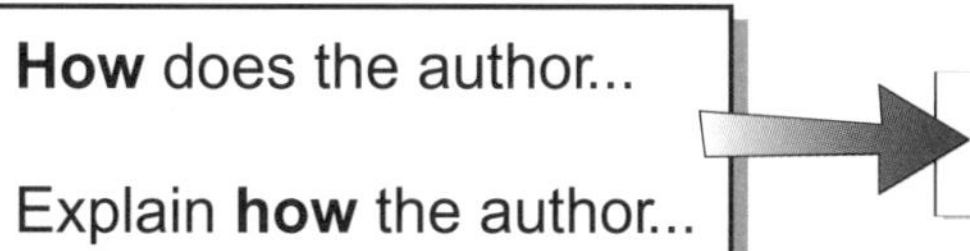

The author creates a spooky atmosphere <u>by</u>...

If the question asks <u>why</u>, use <u>because</u> in your answer:

The author writes in short sentences because...

Follow the instructions and you'll be fine

The trick is <u>not to panic</u>. The question will tell you where to look and how to answer.
Look out for 'how' and 'why' questions — there's more about these on page 34.

Warm-up and Worked Exam Questions

These warm-up questions should help you remember some important advice about the Reading Paper. Get these basics right and you're off to a flying start.

Warm-up Questions

1) What should you do once you've read each bit of writing and all the questions?
   a) Crack on with the first question.
   b) Read the first bit of writing again with the questions in mind.
2) Is this statement true or false?
   "If the question asks for two quotations, try to find more, just to be on the safe side."
3) Read this bit of a story: *"Calvin had dirty fingernails, a runny nose and bits of his breakfast still stuck between his teeth. He kicked viciously at the cat as he left the house."*
   a) Which of the following words describes how the writer wants us to feel about Calvin?
   love **sympathy** **disgust** **admiration**
   b) Which detail tells us that he has a bad temper?
4) A question asks you to explain how a writer creates a feeling of tension in a piece of writing. Which of the following phrases would be the best way to start your answer?
   a) Just like the writer, I hate snakes and...
   b) The writer creates a feeling of tension by...
   c) I disagree with this question because...

Now have a look at these exam-style questions. They've been answered for you, so you can see the sort of things you need to write when you do your exam.

Worked Exam Questions

This is an extract from a ghost story by Ramsey Campbell.
Read it carefully, then answer the questions which follow.

Call First

Through the opening of the door he heard her padding upstairs. She sounded barefoot. Ned waited until he couldn't hear her, then edged out into the hall. The door began to swing open behind him with a faint creak, and he drew it stealthily closed. He paced towards the front door. If he hadn't seen her shadow creeping down the stairs he would have come face to face with her.

1. Where does Ned head for after he reaches the hall?

He goes towards the front door.

Because it's only worth one mark you don't have to write much.

(1 mark)

2. Write down a word in the fourth sentence which shows that Ned doesn't want to be noticed.

Stealthily

(1 mark)

The question says "the fourth sentence" so this is the only word you could use.

Worked Exam Questions

When you get questions asking how or why a writer does something, there's often more than one right answer. Don't worry though — just make sure you do what the question asks. Give reasons for your answer and include examples from the text.

Worked Exam Questions

In this poem, Philip Gross writes about a travelling circus arriving in town.

For One Night Only

The deadbeat circus
rolls up on the hard edge of town.

They're sledge-hammering stakes in, raising
dust and thistledown.

Now they've run up the slack flounce of a tent.
A man barks at the moon.

They've nailed their colours to the sky
just as it darkens. Two bald clowns

come flatfoot, fly-postering everything
that can't get away. The show goes on

and on. Long past bedtime,
the stilt walker stalks through the streets,

face level with your bedroom window.
In the morning, someone will be gone.

1. In line 12, the writer uses a word to describe how the stilt walker moves.

   a) Write the word down.

   stalks

   (1 mark)

   b) What effect does that word have?

   It makes the stilt-walker sound menacing, as if he's hunting something.

   (1 mark)

   You obviously don't have to use these exact words, but you have to get across the idea that the stilt walker sounds dangerous.

2. Explain how the writer involves the reader in the last two lines of the poem.

   The writer involves the reader by saying "your bedroom window." Then when we read the last line "someone will be gone" it seems like a direct threat to us.

   (2 marks)

If a question asks "How?", use the word "by" in your answer.

The question asked you about the last two lines — so make sure you mention both.

Exam Questions

Exam Questions

In this newspaper article the writer reports on how the Titanic, a cruise ship, sank on her first voyage.

The Sinking of the Titanic, 1912

On April 10, 1912, the *Titanic*, largest ship afloat, left Southampton, England on her maiden voyage to New York City. The White Star Line had spared no expense in assuring her luxury. A legend even before she sailed, her passengers were a mixture of the world's wealthiest basking in the elegance of first class accommodations and immigrants packed into steerage.

She was touted as the safest ship ever built, so safe that she carried only 20 lifeboats — enough to provide accommodation for only half her 2,200 passengers and crew. This discrepancy rested on the belief that since the ship's construction made her "unsinkable," her lifeboats were necessary only to rescue survivors of other sinking ships. Additionally, lifeboats took up valuable deck space.

Four days into her journey, at 11:40 P.M. on the night of April 14, she struck an iceberg. Her fireman compared the sound of the impact to "the tearing of calico*, nothing more." However, the collision was fatal and the icy water soon poured through the ship.

It became obvious that many would not find safety in a lifeboat. Each passenger was issued a life jacket but life expectancy would be short when exposed to water four degrees below freezing. As the forward portion of the ship sank deeper, passengers scrambled to the stern. John Thayer witnessed the sinking from a lifeboat. "We could see groups of the almost fifteen hundred people still aboard, clinging in clusters or bunches, like swarming bees; only to fall in masses, pairs or singly, as the great after part of the ship, two hundred and fifty feet of it, rose into the sky, till it reached a sixty-five or seventy degree angle." The great ship slowly slid beneath the waters two hours and forty minutes after the collision.

The next morning, the liner *Carpathia* rescued 705 survivors. One thousand five hundred and twenty-two passengers and crew were lost. Subsequent inquiries attributed the high loss of life to an insufficient number of lifeboats and inadequate training in their use.

* calico = a type of cloth

Exam Questions

Exam Questions

1. From the second paragraph, give two reasons why the Titanic only carried 20 lifeboats.

   ....

   ....

   (2 marks)

2. In paragraph one, the writer contrasts the wealthy passengers with the poor ones. Pick out two phrases from this paragraph which show this contrast.

   ....

   ....

   (2 marks)

3. In paragraph three we are told that when the ship struck the iceberg, the fireman on board compared the sound to "the tearing of calico". Explain what this phrase implies about how serious the collision sounded to the fireman.

   ....

   ....

   ....

   (2 marks)

4. In paragraph four, an eyewitness in a lifeboat uses a simile to describe the people left on board as the ship sinks.

   a) Write down the simile.

   ....

   (1 mark)

   Remember, a simile is a comparison that uses "like" or "as".

   b) Explain the effect this simile has on the reader.

   ....

   ....

   (1 mark)

How Much to Write

This page is all about making sure you do just the right amount to get the marks.
Write too much and you're wasting time. Write too little, and you definitely won't get full marks.

*Look at the **Number of Marks***

At the bottom of each question it tells you how many marks you can get for it.
Short questions are worth 1 mark, 2 marks or 3 marks.

1) For a 1 mark question you only need to make one point, find one phrase or give one word.

2) If the question's worth 2 marks you'll need to have two bits to your answer.

3) For 3 mark questions you'll need to make three points — you won't get three marks for a one-word answer.

*The **Answer Space** Shows You **How Much** to Write*

The space for writing your answer gives you a massive clue about how much you should write.

If the lines go all the way across the page write a sentence.

- *Feeding soup to goblins can make them implode.*
- *Giving soup to goblins reminds them of the war.*

When they give you bullet points, put one point for each.

If there's just a small space, write in notes, or give a one-word answer.

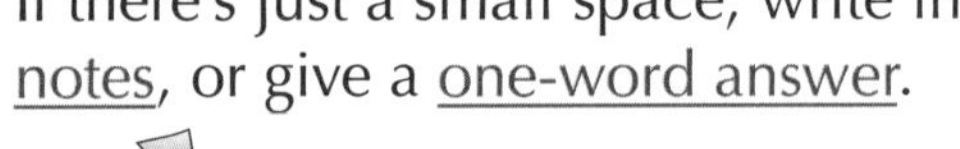

implosion

For grids it's OK to write in note form. Write something in all the empty boxes.

	Goblins	Trolls
Author's attitude	*thinks they're disgusting*	*admires trolls*
Phrase showing author's attitude	*"fetid stench"*	*"superhuman strength"*

Make sure your answer fits into the space given — if you end up trying to squeeze it in with really small writing, you're writing too much.

If your answer hardly fills the space at all then something's gone a bit wrong.
You've probably missed something in the piece you had to read. Have another look at it.

It's important to write the right amount

The stuff on this page is easy to remember. Just two simple things — write enough to get the marks, and use all the space they give you for writing your answers.

Mini-Essay Questions

The last question for some texts is a bit longer. You have to do a little mini-essay.

The *Mini-Essay* Questions Look Like This

These questions ask about the whole text — don't get stuck in the first couple of paragraphs. Make sure you write about the whole thing.

In the whole text, how does the author mix horror and humour?

You should comment on:
- how the author describes the main character
- how the author describes the fight scenes
- whether you think there is more horror or humour in the story

(5 marks)

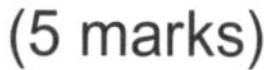

If they give you prompts, use them to organise your answer. Write about each one in turn.

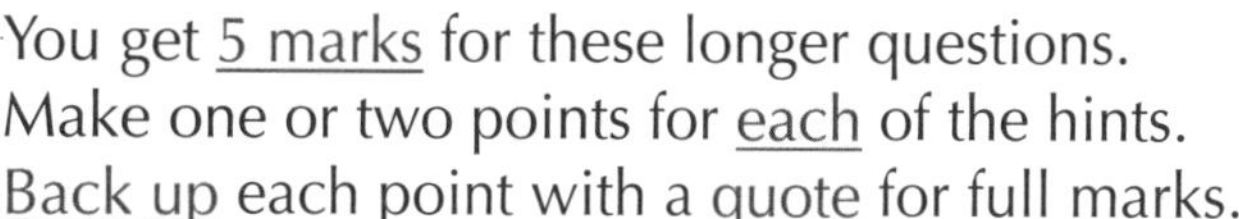

You get 5 marks for these longer questions. Make one or two points for each of the hints. Back up each point with a quote for full marks.

You won't always get prompts. If you don't, you should still aim to have at least three main chunks to your answer.

Don't Spend Ages on the Long Questions

These mini-essays will take a bit longer to do than the shorter questions. Obviously. But you don't have time to muck about.

1) Go back to the piece you've read. Pick out the bits you're going to write about — underline the bits that answer the question, or put stars in the margin.

2) Once you start writing don't do anything fancy. Stick to clear, simple English. Make a point, back it up with a quote, and move on to your next point. Keep going till you've made at least 5 decent points.

3) Have a quick read through what you've written to make sure you haven't said anything that's obviously wrong.

4) Go on to the next question.

The main thing is not to get bogged down. If you really dry up on one of these questions, leave it. Do all the short questions first, then come back at the end.

Mini-essay questions aren't as hard as they look

These questions are a bit harder than the short questions. But not that much harder. Don't spend all your valuable test time on just one long question, or you'll mess up the rest of the test.

What Questions Mean

If you want to write a good answer, you'd better make sure that you understand the question.

Work Out What the Question **Wants You to Do**

Sometimes, the questions aren't quite as straightforward as they might be.
But those hard-looking questions actually just want you to do a few not-so-hard things.

Look at these questions — and see what they really want you to do.

Q. How is suspense created in this story?

1) Write about the events that happen in the story which create suspense.
2) Write about the words that the writer uses to create suspense.
3) Write about the way the story is put together — does the writer leave some things out to make you wonder what's going on?

Don't Try to do **Everything** at Once

Break the question down into easy bits before you try to answer it.

Say what the writer tells readers about the castle.

Write about the words the writer chooses to make the castle seem interesting.

Q. In what way does the article make you want to visit the castle?

Write about the way the writer ends the article — does the writer decide that the castle is worth visiting?

Exam questions aren't all that complicated

It's easy to fall into the trap of over-complicating exam questions. If the question looks tricky, take a deep breath, read it again, and think about what it's asking. This makes it much easier.

What Questions Mean

Different questions want you to do different things. Here are some things to look out for.

Look out for **Key Words** in the Question

Work out what kind of question it is. These key words are a massive clue.

Q. How does the writer...

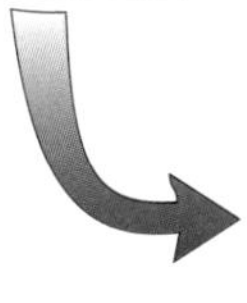

You always have to talk about the words the writer uses and the way the piece is put together for this kind of question.

Q. How does the writer build up a picture of...

Talk about the words the writer uses. If it's a story, talk about the reactions of the narrator and the characters.

Q. What is your impression of the shopkeeper?

Write about what kind of person the shopkeeper is. Say which bits you've used to get your answer.

The words are the key to the question

The words in exam questions are all there for a reason. If you can work out exactly what a question is asking you, you're half-way to writing a good answer.

Different Questions

Different questions need answering in different ways.
It's worth looking out for key words in the question to help you decide how to answer it.

Make Your Answer **Fit The Question**

1) Different questions can ask about the same thing in different ways.

2) Don't fall into the trap of thinking, "This is a question about horses, so I'll just write down everything I know about horses".

3) You really have to look for those key words — they tell you what the question wants you to do.

The **Wording** Affects **How** you **Tackle** the Question

Both the questions below basically mean "write about the supervisor at the doorknob factory" — but you need to tackle them in slightly different ways.

Q. What impression do you get of the supervisor at the doorknob factory?

The key words in this question are "What impression". This is a simple, open question. It's asking you to comment on what the supervisor says and does.

The key words here are "How does the writer". This is a bit more specific. You need to write about the writer's use of language.

Q. How does the writer make you dislike the supervisor at the doorknob factory?

You also get a handy hint with this question — the word "dislike". You know you're looking for things that show the supervisor in a bad light.

Different Questions

So now you know that the wording of questions can affect how you should answer them. Here's a couple of ideas of how you can put this into practice.

How to Make Your Answer Fit the Question

Here's what you might do differently to answer the two questions on the previous page. Both answers talk about the same thing, but from slightly different angles.

Q. What impression do you get of the supervisor at the doorknob factory?

The supervisor of the doorknob factory treats the workers badly. She thinks they are useless, and keeps threatening them with the sack.

This answer talks about what the writer says in the story.

Like a chef deciding what to cook.

Q. How does the writer make you dislike the supervisor at the doorknob factory?

The writer spends a long time describing how the supervisor treats her workers. The writer uses words like "yells", "threatened" and "a sarcastic laugh" to show that the supervisor speaks to the workers in a cruel way.

This answer talks about how the writer says it.

This is about choice of words and structure.

Like a chef deciding how to cook it.

Spot the difference

The differences between one kind of question and another can be subtle. But if you pick up on exactly what it's asking before you start your answer, you'll get precious extra marks.

Warm-up and Worked Exam Questions

Have a go at these questions to help you remember some key points about the Reading Paper.

Warm-up Questions

1) When you're wondering how much to write for an answer, which two things give you the best clues?
2) What should you do if you get stuck on the mini-essay question?
3) If a mini-essay question says "You should comment on these points", what does it mean?
   a) You should, but don't stress if you can't, we understand it's not easy.
   b) You have to comment on everything listed here if you want to get full marks.
4) You're allowed to write on the question paper. What would it be useful to underline to help you get your answer ready?
5) 'How' is a word which you often see in questions. Choose three things you might need to write about if you see the word 'how' in a question.
   a) The details in the text.
   b) The words a writer uses.
   c) How many cups of coffee you think the writer needed to get started.
   d) The way the story is put together — a strong beginning or ending for example, or the order of events.

Worked Exam Question

This article about waste disposal is from *The Guardian* newspaper.

This week the subject's a load of old rubbish — 435 million tonnes of it, in fact. That's the amount of waste products that need to be got rid of every year in this country. What to do with all this waste is a big headache. The two most common solutions are to bury it or burn it. The first approach relies on giving large areas over to what is known as landfill. The other involves incinerating (burning) the waste at extremely high temperatures.

The trouble is that landfill sites are few and far between, and because we produce so much waste they quickly fill up. One of the biggest in Europe is located at a place called Packingham near Birmingham and it will only be able to accept new loads of waste for the next eight years.

On the other hand, incinerators may take up much less room but they are not popular with local people as they release pollution and have been associated with producing highly dangerous chemicals called dioxins.

This means you have to write something in every box in the table. Don't leave any blanks.

1. Complete the table below with details of the main problems of using landfill sites and incinerators.

	Problem One	Problem Two
Landfill sites	*There aren't many of them.*	*They fill up quickly.*
Incinerators	*Locals don't like them.*	*They produce pollution and dioxins.*

(2 marks)

Worked Exam Questions

Mini-essay questions will expect you to make several different points about a text and back them up with quotes. Take a look at how this example answer has used the hints in the question.

Worked Exam Question

First Ice *by Andrei Voznesensky*

In the telephone booth a girl
is turning into ice.
Huddled in a thin coat
her face is tear-stained
and smeared with lipstick.

She wears earrings made out of glass
and breathes on fingers that freeze.
She will have to go home now.
Alone along the icy street.

First frost. A beginning of losses.
The first frost of telephone phrases.
Winter glistens on her cheek.
The first frost of having been hurt.

1. How does the writer make us feel that the girl in the poem is unhappy?
In your answer you should comment on:
- the details he gives us
- the language he uses
- the way the poem is set out

Make sure you cover all of these pointers.

Back your points up with quotes and examples.

The writer makes us feel that the girl in the poem is unhappy by using a mixture of facts and descriptive language. One detail is that her face is "tear stained" which shows she has just been crying. He also finishes the poem with the line "The first frost of having been hurt" which tells us clearly that something has just caused her pain.

The language he uses links the coldness she is feeling inside with the coldness outside. On line 2 he says she "is turning into ice". This means that she is not only getting colder as she stands in the telephone box but that what she has been told has made her emotionally frozen with shock. The word "huddled" makes her seem vulnerable and miserable.

The poem is set out in short lines and stanzas which makes it seem bleak and comfortless. The lines seem to stand alone like the girl does. Words like "alone" and "hurt" are emphasised by being at the beginning or the end of a line.

(5 marks)

Exam Questions

This is what the question in your exam will be like. It might not look like much fun, but if you get some practice in now, you'll feel much more confident when you have to answer one of these for real.

Exam Questions

In this extract from *Nicholas Nickleby* by Charles Dickens, Nicholas has come to teach at Dotheboys Hall. Here the Headmaster, Mr Squeers, shows him the schoolroom and the pupils for the first time.

By degrees, the place resolved itself into a bare and dirty room with a couple of windows whereof a tenth part might be of glass, the remainder being stopped up with old copy-books and paper. There were a couple of long old rickety desks, cut and notched and inked and damaged, in every possible way; two or three forms, a detached desk for Squeers and another for his assistant. The ceiling was supported like that of a barn, by cross beams and rafters, and the walls were so stained and discoloured, that it was impossible to tell whether they had ever been touched with paint or whitewash.

But the pupils — the young noblemen! The last faint traces of hope, the remotest glimmering of any good to be derived in this den, faded from the mind of Nicholas as he looked in dismay around! Pale and haggard faces, lank and bony figures, children with the countenances of old men, deformities with irons upon their limbs, boys of stunted growth, and others whose long meagre legs would hardly bear their stooping bodies, all crowded on the view together; there were the bleared eye, the hare lip, the crooked foot, and every other ugliness or distortion that told of un-natural aversion conceived by parents for their offspring, or of young lives which, from the earliest dawn of infancy, had been one horrible endurance of cruelty and neglect. There were little faces which should have been handsome, darkened with the scowl of sullen suffering; there was childhood with the light of its eye quenched, its beauty gone and its helplessness alone remaining.

Exam Questions

Exam Questions

1. What impression do you get of the schoolroom from the first paragraph?

....

....

....

(2 marks)

2. Write down two phrases from the second paragraph which tell us clearly that the boys have been badly treated.

....

....

....

(2 marks)

3. How does the writer give us a strong sense of how dreadful this school is?
You should comment on:

- the kind of details he includes
- the words he uses
- the length of the sentences

....

....

....

....

....

....

....

....

....

....

(5 marks)

Questions About Language

When they ask questions about the language, you have to write about the words that a writer chooses to describe things. This page shows you what to do, so learn it.

Write about **Descriptions**

If you're asked how a writer creates a picture of something, you'll have to write about the words that he or she uses to describe it.

> The rustling noise grew louder and more persistent. When it started, Marcie had thought of leaves blowing in the wind, but now it was far too loud for that. It sounded like someone stomping through crisp packets. The rustling turned into crunching, as if some huge animal was munching on a gigantic cream cracker.

The bits in blue give you an idea of a really loud crunching sound.

Does the Writer **Finish** the Description all in **One Go**?

1) Often, a writer won't describe the thing they're talking about all in one go.
2) This often happens in stories when a new character or place is introduced to the reader — the writer tells you about them a bit at a time.
3) If you notice this, write about it in your answer. It'll get you more marks.

Write about **Words** Used to Create a **Mood**

Questions that ask things like "How does the writer build up tension?" look rather nasty. First of all, you need to find words that give you an idea of tension or alarm. Then see how the writer increases the fear and alarm felt by the narrator and the characters in the story.

> *At first, the narrator is "slightly suspicious" of the man in the green jumper. The writer builds up the narrator's feeling of alarm as she realises that the man is up to no good. She becomes "more and more afraid". The writer describes the narrator's fear when she thinks the man has seen her. This creates tension. The tension is kept up right until the man leaves the museum.*

There's a reason for everything

Nothing in the writing is the way it is by accident. The writer has chosen words deliberately to make the readers feel happy, or sad, or tense, or excited or whatever.

Structure

If you're asked about how the writer does something in the story, it's always worth writing about how the piece is actually put together. It won't have been written that way by accident.

*Are the **Beginning** and **End** Different?*

You might be asked about this in the exam, so pay attention.
Sometimes the very end of a piece is written in a slightly different style to create an effect.

For example, when a writer is trying to persuade readers, he or she might round the piece off by talking in a direct and friendly way about his or her own experience.

Non-fiction articles that start with a question of some sort will end by answering the question. This rounds the article off nicely.

In conclusion, we can answer the question posed at the beginning of this article by saying that criminals should be rehabilitated as well as punished.

*Does the Writer seem to **Change** his or her **Opinion**?*

Underwater Snooker by Ted Hanson

In the last few years, many bizarre new sports like pogo-stick racing and tree surfing have taken off.

One that seems unlikely to ever become popular is underwater snooker. I must admit, I laughed out loud when the idea was first suggested to me. I couldn't imagine why anyone would want to put on a wetsuit and climb into a swimming pool for a game of snooker.

I was invited to Sharky's Pool and Snooker Pool, and after a couple of games I was hooked. The experience of potting a ball six feet underwater is something that has to be tried.

The writer has changed his mind. He's decided he likes underwater snooker.

It isn't that the writer can't make his mind up here. He's actually changing his opinion on purpose. He starts off by saying that underwater snooker is crazy — that's something that most readers would agree with. Then he says that he's been convinced by a visit to a snooker pool. He wants readers to agree with him here, too.

The structure is really important

For these "how does the writer?" type of questions, the way that the piece is put together is as important as the words the writer uses. Remember — the writer did it that way on purpose.

Questions Asking for Your Opinion

Some questions ask you specifically for what you think.
This is another kind of question that you need to tackle in a slightly different way.

Watch Out For Questions That Want Your *Opinion*

It's normally a bad idea to write "I think" or "in my opinion" in your Reading Paper answers. The only time you should is if the question specifically asks what you think.

These two questions are very similar, but you'll get more marks for tackling them differently.

In what ways does the article try to persuade people to watch more movies?

Write about what the article says and how it says it.

The key words are "do you think".

Do you think the article will persuade people to watch more movies?

With this question you need to write about what the article says, how it says it, AND say how effective you think it is.

How to *Answer* Opinion Questions

There's no big secret about answering questions that ask what you think.
You just have to remember to give reasons for what you think. These can be pretty much the same things you would write to answer a normal question.

In what ways does the article try to persuade people to watch more movies?

The article says that watching movies is a good way to escape from real life for a couple of hours.

This answer talks about a point the article makes.

Do you think the article will persuade people to watch more movies?

I think it will persuade people because everyone needs to forget their troubles for a couple of hours every now and then.

This says that you think it's a good point — and it says why you think so.

Only give your opinion if you're asked for it

Opinion questions are great — you get to say what you think. Just make sure you give reasons, or you'll be throwing marks away. Only give your opinion if the question asks you to.

Finding the Important Bits

The hard thing is finding the bit of the writing that tells you the answer to the question.

Find the **Bits that Answer** the *Question*

Q. In what way does the article make readers want to visit the Castle?

The key to answering questions like this is to find loads of things in the article that help answer the question. Here's the start of the article with the bits you need and the bits you don't need helpfully pointed out...

Callendale Castle, often called one of the finest castles in England, is built on a hill overlooking the village of Callendale in West Bassetshire. On approaching Callendale village, the twin towers of the castle suddenly loomed through the mist, giving the village a mysterious appearance.

Callendale Castle holds many stories, and many secrets. A quick read through the guidebook gave me a colourful insight into the way things must have been inside these forbidding stone walls all those years ago. A secret meeting between King Henry V and a French ambassador took place here during the Hundred Years War. In 1814, the castle narrowly escaped being burnt to the ground when a lazy kitchen boy left a pig roasting on the open fire unattended.

The castle tour took me to a dark, dank dungeon, complete with gruesome instruments of torture. Hidden in one corner is a tiny cell, little more than a hole, where countless prisoners were left to rot away. It is hard to imagine how a grown person could fit into a space so small.

Next, the Armoury Museum conjured up the blood and excitement of a medieval battle. During my visit, a party of schoolchildren were gleefully discussing which of the various gleaming swords they would prefer to have their heads chopped off with — which put me right off my lunch.

You DON'T need to say where the castle is.

Mention that it looks mysterious — that makes it sound interesting.

People would want to visit to find out more about the stories and secrets.

You DON'T need to retell these stories in your answer. Just say that the writer mentions them.

The writer spends some time talking about the dungeon. People find horrible things fascinating, so this bit is important.

This bit shows the schoolchildren enjoyed visiting the castle.

There'll be a **Lot** *of Things That* **Aren't Important**

There'll always be a great load of stuff that's got nothing to do with the question. Don't write about every tiny little thing — only write about the bits that the question asks for.

You have to judge which bits are important

Nobody can teach you to pick out the important bits. You have to make sure you go through the text and get all the important bits out. Remember — not all of it will be important.

Question Pointers

This is a massively important page. Face it, losing a whole grade because you didn't read the question properly would be pretty embarrassing. Don't let it happen — learn this page.

Always Use the **Question Pointers**

Often a question will be followed by some pointers telling you what to put in your answer. Whatever you do, don't ignore these pointers. They're much more than helpful hints from the examiners — they're your ticket to better marks. You'd have to be mad to ignore them.

When it says "you should" it means you absolutely must do this.

> **How does the writer try to make you feel sympathy for Mr Hobscuttle?**
>
> In your answer you should comment on:
> - the way his childhood is described
> - the way the supervisor at the doorknob factory treats him
> - the way his relationship with his wife changes

Write about all of these things.

If you write two half-decent paragraphs about each of these three points, you'll get better marks than if you write a brilliant long answer that only talks about one of them.

Write About **All** of the **Points**

Don't miss any of the points out. Write about all of them.
If you forget to write about one of the points, you will lose marks, and that's guaranteed.
Your mark could actually go down a whole level — a seriously hefty drop.

Try to spend a roughly equal amount of time talking about each of the pointers they give you. It doesn't have to be exact, but it shouldn't be far off.

Ignore the pointers at your peril

You either learn this or you've had it, basically. When the question says "You should comment on..." it really means "You must write about...". Every year, people lose out on easy marks because they don't follow what the question says. Don't be one of them.

Writing Your Answer

You need to know how to put your answer together. Once again, it's all about getting the best possible marks for your answer. So, it looks like you need to get this page learned.

Start by Saying **How** you **Answer** the Question

It's a good idea to give a little introduction to your answer. All it needs to do is say what your basic answer to the question is. It helps the examiner to see that you're setting off in the right direction, so it'll help you get more marks.

This is the basic idea of your answer.

The writer makes us feel sympathy for Mr Hobscuttle by describing his life as unhappy. The writer shows us that other people are to blame for Mr Hobscuttle's misfortune.

Go Through **All** of the **Points** in Turn

The question pointers actually make it a lot easier to put your answer together. Write about each of the points in turn. It really is that simple.

Write about one point...

Mr Hobscuttle "always tried in vain" to please his father, which tells us that his father was never happy with anything he did. His parents didn't show him love...

...and then go on to the next.

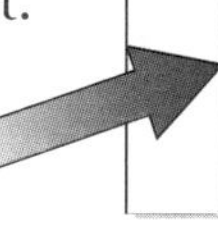

Linking phrases like this show where your answer is going.

Another person who treats Mr Hobscuttle badly is the supervisor at the doorknob factory. She...

Make it **Obvious** that You're **Answering** the **Question**

Don't be afraid to be blatant and repeat phrases directly from the question. It makes the examiner notice that you've read the question carefully and you're doing your best to answer it.

Of course, you can't just leave it at that — you have to go on and write more about each point.

Another area of Mr Hobscuttle's life where the writer tries to make us feel sympathy for him is the way his relationship with his wife changes. For example, the writer says...

This bit comes from the question.

Only take phrases, not huge chunks, or the examiner will think you're just copying it from the question and don't know what you're talking about (see page 53).

Question pointers make your life easier

The idea here is that you use the question pointers to help you write a good answer. They're like a ready-made plan. Write about them in order, and there you go, one well-structured answer.

Warm-up and Worked Exam Questions

You've reached the end of the first section — well done. Before you take a break, work your way through these pages to test how much you've learnt. First off there's some warm-up questions about the stuff on the last few pages.

Warm-up Questions

1) Which of the following statements are true?
   a) Writers don't choose the words they use with a particular purpose in mind.
   b) You don't have to make your answer fit the question.
   c) It's important to give relevant details to back-up your answers.
   d) You should use the pointers that follow the questions.
   e) It's a good idea to begin longer answers with a brief introduction.
   f) It's not a good idea to repeat phrases from the question in your answer.

Here's an example of a Reading Question. Read the extract carefully and then read through the questions which follow on the next page, paying close attention to the answers.

Worked Exam Question

This extract is from 'Zlata's Diary'. Zlata was an 11 year-old girl who kept a diary of the events she witnessed during the war in former Yugoslavia in the 1990s.

Zlata's Diary

Monday, 6th April 1992

Dear Mimmy,

Yesterday the people in front of the parliament tried peacefully to cross the Vrbanja bridge. But they were shot at. Who? How? Why? A girl, a medical student from Dubrovnik, was KILLED. Her blood was spilled onto the bridge. In her final moments all she said was: "Is this Sarajevo?"

HORRIBLE, HORRIBLE, HORRIBLE!

The Bascarsija has been destroyed! Those "fine gentlemen" from Pale fired on Bascarsija!

Since yesterday people have been inside the B-H parliament. Some of them are standing outside, in front of it. We've moved my television set into the living room, so I watch Channel 1 on one TV and Good Vibrations on the other. Now they're shooting from the Holiday Inn, killing people in front of the parliament. And Bokica is there with Vanja and Andrej. Oh, God!

Maybe we'll go to the cellar. You, Mimmy, will go with me, of course. I'm desperate. The people in front of the parliament are desperate too. Mimmy, war is here.

PEACE, NOW !

They say they're going to attack RTV Sarajevo. But they haven't. They've stopped shooting in our neighbourhood. KNOCK! KNOCK! (I'm knocking on wood for good luck.)

WHEW! That was close. Oh, God! They're shooting again!!!

Zlata

* Bascarsija = a market square in Sarajevo

** B-H = Bosnia-Herzegovina

Worked Exam Questions

Here are some typical Reading Questions based on the extract from 'Zlata's Diary'. First read the questions and then re-read the extract. Look closely at the sample answers to pick up some useful points for the exam paper.

Worked Exam Questions

1. The diary is addressed to 'Dear Mimmy'. Why does Zlata give the diary a name?

She calls the diary 'Mimmy' because she treats it like a close friend.

(1 mark)

2. Pick out a phrase from the extract that shows that Zlata is writing as if she is speaking to a friend.

Just writing the phrase is enough.

"You, Mimmy, will go with me, of course."

(1 mark)

3. What effect do the words printed in capitals have on the tone of the text?

They make the tone of the text more dramatic — as if the writer is shouting.

(1 mark)

Remember to state the obvious — it's often all the question is looking for.

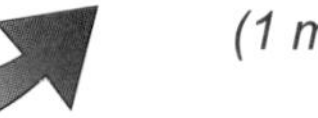

4. Why do you think the writer uses inverted commas to refer to the "fine gentlemen" from Pale?

The use of inverted commas shows that the writer is being sarcastic. The men who have destroyed Bascarsija are not "fine" or "gentlemen" if they have been that violent.

You need to explain your answer to get the second mark.

(2 marks)

5. How does the writer involve the reader in her story?

The writer involves the reader by writing in an informal, chatty style. For example when she writes, "WHEW! That was close". She also involves the reader by providing dramatic details of what has happened, e.g. "A girl, a medical student from Dubrovnik, was KILLED." She makes the writing seem exciting by using capital letters and exclamation marks. She also involves the reader by revealing her personal fears, e.g. "KNOCK! KNOCK! (I'm knocking on wood for good luck.)"

(4 marks)

Remember to back up your points with a quote or example — it'll improve your marks.

Exam Questions

In the SATs you will be given a Reading Question where you have to compare two texts on the same theme. The following two texts are both on the subject of homelessness.

Exam Questions

'Stone Cold' by Robert Swindells

Link is a homeless teenager living on the streets of London.

So you pick your spot. Wherever it is (unless you're in a squat or a derelict house or something) it's going to have a floor of stone, tile concrete or brick. In other words it's going to be hard and cold... Settled for the night? Well maybe, maybe not. Remember my first night? The Scouser? 'Course you do. He kicked me out of my bedroom and pinched my watch. Well, that sort of thing can happen any night, and there are worse things... You might be spotted by a gang of lager louts on the look-out for someone to maim. That happens all the time too, and if they get carried away you can end up dead. There are the guys who like young boys, who think because you're a dosser you'll do anything for dosh and there's the psycho who'll knife you for your pack.

So you lie listening. You bet you do. Footsteps. Voices. Breathing, even. Doesn't help you sleep.

And those are only some of the hassles. I haven't mentioned stomach cramps from hunger, headaches from the flu, toothache, fleas and lice. I haven't talked about homesickness, depression or despair.

University of York press release, 5th March 2003

A new report published today in partnership with the National Missing Persons Helpline charity presents the findings of the most extensive study of missing persons ever undertaken in the UK. It found that going missing was highly risky for young people. Almost a third stayed with a stranger and 2 out of 5 slept rough. 1 in 8 was physically hurt and 1 in 9 sexually assaulted when they were away.

The study...also found that over a third of young people had no help at all while they were away. Only a minority felt they were happier than they had been before they ran away.

Despite the risks involved, nearly half reported that they had not attempted to seek help while they were missing.

"Running away never helps people solve their problems. I realised that when it was too late...If you meet the right people you will be OK, like I was, but most of the time you end up sleeping rough. They should have people that talk to us, so we can clear it out, because in our eyes the only way out is to run away."

Exam Questions

Keep checking the texts on page 28 when answering these questions.

1. Write out a phrase from 'Stone Cold' that is written in informal language.

....

(1 mark)

2. Why do you think the writer of 'Stone Cold' lists all the "hassles" of living rough?

....

....

(2 marks)

3. Why do you think the University of York Press Release includes a quotation from a homeless teenager?

....

....

(2 marks)

4. Both texts highlight the dangers of living on the streets for young people.
How effective is each piece in showing the reader the dangers?
You should talk about the following in your answer:

- the dangers involved
- the views of both writers
- the language used in the texts

....

....

....

....

....

....

....

....

....

....

....

....

(5 Marks)

Revision Summary Questions

Well done, you've made it to the end of the section. There's quite a lot to get to grips with here, and you need to know it all. The best way to make sure you know everything in this section is to go through these questions over and over again until you're absolutely sure that you know all the answers. If you don't, you can go back and check. Remember, the whole point of revision is to find out what you don't know, and then learn it until you do.

1) Name three Golden Rules about Reading Questions.
2) Sarah says you shouldn't read the piece of writing first, but should skip straight to the questions. Is she right?
3) Is it OK to say simple, obvious things in your answers?
4) How does pretending the examiners don't know anything get you better marks?
5) Should you bother being neat?
6) Are questions that ask you what's going on:
   a) very easy
   b) horrendous and not to be attempted
   c) straightforward, so long as you read the question carefully?
7) For questions about style is it best to go into lots of detail or be nice and vague?
8) Do short questions tell you where to look for the answer?
9) If the question says "Write down 4 phrases..." should you write down:
   a) up to 4 phrases b) at least 4 phrases c) exactly 4 phrases?
10) Should you normally answer "how" questions with "by" or "because"?
11) Should you normally answer "why" questions with "by" or "because"?
12) If a question's worth 2 marks, how many bits are they expecting in your answer?
13) If you haven't got enough space to write your answer, what should you do?
14) Do the mini-essay questions ask about the odd paragraph, or the whole piece of writing?
15) Do you always get helpful hints on the mini-essay questions?
16) What would be different about your answers to these two questions?
   a) What impressions do you get of the giant mongoose?
   b) How does the writer make you like the giant mongoose?
17) When you get a question about how a piece of writing describes something or makes a picture of something, what do you need to look for so you can give an answer?
18) What's the important thing to do for questions that ask you what you think about something?
19) Is it better to write about all the "in your answer you should comment on" points in a question, or to write a whole load about one or two of them?
20) How can you make it obvious that you're answering the question?

Example — The Story

In the Reading Paper, you get a story to read, then some questions based on the story.

Read the story on this page and the next. Then we'll have a look at the kind of questions you'll have to answer.

In this extract, Jerry Derryberry has turned his unsuccessful bakery into a thriving business by selling skateboards for dogs.

Jerry Derryberry was sound asleep when the alarm clock chirped. He was awake in an instant, feeling bright and alert, not like in the old days when he had to struggle to rouse himself from a deep and dreamy slumber.

"Good morning, Kerry," he said cheerfully as he walked into the kitchen, where his wife was busy frying artichokes for breakfast. "Oh no," thought Jerry, "not artichokes again." He'd much rather just have a nice piece of toast. Jerry had been dropping hints for over a week now that he didn't like fried artichokes, but Kerry hadn't noticed. "I'd be quite happy with toast, you know, love."

"*Know Your Vegetables* magazine says the ancient Egyptians considered fried artichokes to be a source of health and strength," Kerry replied humourlessly, bringing two large plates of steaming artichokes to the table. Jerry groaned inwardly. In the past he might have got into an argument with Kerry about her silly magazines, but he was so happy at the success of his shop that he was much more able to cope with her these days.

"Those are bags under your eyes," Kerry said. "You should be sleeping more."

Jerry smiled patiently. "Don't be silly love," he said, "I sleep much more than you do."

Jerry was glad when breakfast was over and it was time to go to work. He positively bounced and skipped the ten minute walk to his shop, so full of energy was he feeling. The door to Jerry's bakery was open, and he could smell the sweet aroma of freshly baking bread. He filled his lungs and beamed with pride to think that this little shop, from which he had struggled to make a living for so long, was now beginning to build him an empire.

"Hello, Wayne," he called. "That smells wonderful. Will you be okay here in the shop while I check on the skateboard factory?"

"Sure thing, boss," Wayne responded. He was delighted to do anything the boss asked, since Jerry had given him that big pay rise.

Jerry closed the shop door behind him and went next door into the factory, which had been a dusty, long-deserted warehouse until he bought it and started manufacturing skateboards for dogs.

Example — The Story

As he closed the factory door behind him and surveyed the dozens of workers busily crafting pooch-sized skateboards, Jerry reflected on how long it had taken him to strike it lucky with one of his inventions. He used to sit at his desk until the early hours of the morning, tired after a long day at work, dreaming up ideas. He'd tried sleeping bags for fish, kangaroo binoculars, jigsaws for gerbils. None had caught on. But finally, he reflected, all those years of enterprise and hard work had paid off.

"What are you working on, Lisa?" he asked his chief designer.

"A new model for poodles," Lisa replied cheerfully. "We have to adapt our other designs because poodles have such small paws."

"Good, good," Jerry smiled benevolently. "Keep up the good work."

Jerry went back into the shop, where Wayne was serving a customer — a big-boned, jolly looking man who had a small, yapping white dog on a leash.

"I'm sorry, sir," Wayne was saying, "but none of our skateboards are suitable for poodles."

The man looked crestfallen. Smoothly, Jerry stepped in to assure him that a new model for poodles was being designed as he spoke. The customer's face brightened and the poodle, perhaps sensing his owner's mood, yapped happily. Jerry spent a moment thinking how wonderful it was that his idea had brought such pleasure into people's lives. Every day he saw customers' smiling faces in his shop, and it always gave him a warm glow of satisfaction.

"That's wonderful," the man said. "Oh, and I'll have a medium-sliced wholemeal loaf while I'm here, please."

Wayne extracted a freshly-baked wholemeal loaf from behind the counter and put it into the slicing machine. Meanwhile, an elderly lady walked in and looked in confusion at the display of dog skateboards lined up on the shelves. Jerry put a considerate arm around her and asked if she needed any help.

"I thought this was a bakery," she said. "I only wanted a nice sticky bun. I'm eighty-seven, you know." Jerry gave her a bun.

"There you are, my dear," he said. "You can have it for free."

From Derryberry's Dream Comes True, by I. O. Silver

Shorter Questions

Right, you've read the story. The first questions you'll have to answer will be quite short. They put in questions like the ones on this page to test your understanding of the story.

Show You **Understand** the **Story**

The easiest questions of all ask you what's going on.

From paragraph 6 on page 31 write down how long it took Jerry to walk to work.

Jerry was glad when breakfast was over and it was time to go to work. He positively bounced and skipped the ten minute walk to his shop...

There's the answer. Stop reading and write it down. It really is as simple as that.

Some questions need a bit more work. You have to explain things from the story.

From paragraph 1 on page 32, explain why Jerry is happier now than he was in the past.

The answer isn't obvious. You need to work it out. These are the bits that tell you the answer.

...dozens of workers busily crafting pooch-sized skateboards...

...used to sit at his desk until the early hours of the morning...

The answer doesn't have to be fancy or complicated to get the marks.
It just has to be based on the story. You could write:

In the past Jerry used to work hard without getting any results. Now he has dozens of people working for him, putting his ideas into practice.

In **Non-Fiction** Writing You'll Have to Find **Facts**

You won't always get stories to read. They quite often put in articles from magazines, or leaflets and advertisements. For non-fiction they'll ask you to find facts, e.g.

From paragraph 3, write down two benefits of seedless jam.

From paragraph 7, write down one advantage and one disadvantage of selling jam in paper bags.

You answer these in exactly the same way — look at the paragraph, find as many points as they're asking for, and write them down.

Keep it simple

These short questions shouldn't cause too many headaches. Everything you need is in the text.

Shorter Questions

These questions are about style. They test your ability to see what fancy tricks the author's up to.

Go into **Detail** on **Style Questions**

1) This question sounds vague and general — but you can't give a wishy-washy answer.

   In the first paragraph, how does the writer show that Jerry enjoys life?

2) A good answer needs to go into detail about the story.
   Read through the paragraph again, looking for individual words that tell you Jerry is happy.

   Jerry Derryberry was sound asleep when the alarm clock chirped. He was awake in an instant, feeling bright and alert, not like in the old days when he had to struggle to rouse himself from a deep and dreamy slumber.

3) Then explain how each word or phrase adds to the picture of Jerry as a man who enjoys life.

   In the first sentence, the writer says the alarm clock "chirped". Alarm clocks usually make a horrible noise, and chirping is a pleasant sound, so this starts the story off on a positive note.

   Jerry wakes up quickly, feeling "bright and alert". This suggests he looks forward to his day.

   The writer draws a contrast in the second sentence between the present and the past. In "the old days" Jerry had to "struggle" to get out of bed. Now he wakes up quickly and happily. This contrast emphasises the idea that Jerry enjoys life now.

This looks like a lot of writing about just a few words — but you won't get any marks for just putting a one-sentence answer.

People Often Make **Mistakes** on Style Questions

The writer shows Jerry is happier now than he used to be.

This answer is true enough but it doesn't answer the question. This person's written about the plot when they should have been writing about the way the story's written.

The writer shows Jerry enjoys life by using happy words.

This answer is sort of true too. The trouble is it doesn't go into enough detail to get the marks. If it quoted some actual words from the story it would be much better.

Make sure you go into enough detail

Remember, even though they're short questions, it doesn't mean you can just scrawl a few words. And, as ever, make sure you're directly answering the question.

Mini-Essay Questions

The next six pages are about a longer question.

> Q3. How does the writer describe Jerry's state of mind?
>
> In your answer you should comment on:
> • the way Jerry reacts to his wife
> • how he responds to his workplace
> • the way he treats his employees
> • how he reacts to his customers.

There's loads more that you could write for this one. Luckily, it gives you some pointers so you know which bits to concentrate on.

Before you even start to tackle this question, here are three bits of vitally important advice.

1. Write About **All** of Those **Pointers**

When it says "you should comment on," it really means "you must talk about". Those pointers are worth their weight in gold. Read them and use them.

This question tells you to start off by talking about how Jerry behaves with his wife. Then talk about his workplace. Then his employees and then his customers. Try to write a roughly equal amount about each of them.

2. **Think — Why** Did the **Writer** Do it Like This?

Look at the wording of the question. This one starts "how does the writer describe...".

This story isn't just a random collection of thrown together words. It's been deliberately written by an author who wants you to get something out of it.

When you answer the question, think about what the writer was trying to do.

For example, the writer didn't need to mention anything about Jerry's breakfast. The writer could've skipped it and started talking about Jerry at work. The breakfast scene is only there because the writer thinks it will tell us something about Jerry.

3. **Quote** Like You've Never Quoted Before

Quotes show the examiner you've got your answer from the text, not just made it up. More importantly good quotes = good marks. See Section 3 for more on quoting.

Don't be intimidated by mini-essay questions

Don't let the fact that these are longer questions make you think they're impossible. Cover all the pointers, explain in detail and back everything up with quotes and you'll be ok.

Mini-Essay Questions

With those three bits of vital advice bouncing round your head, let's answer the question.

*If You **See** It, **Say** It — Start with **Obvious Points***

You have to start by talking about "the way Jerry reacts to his wife".

Read that section of the story, and write down points as they occur to you. It doesn't matter if they're obvious.

> *The writer says that Jerry greets his wife "cheerfully". This shows he is in a happy state of mind.*

You might think this is so obvious it's hardly worth saying. Actually it's a great way to start your answer.

*It's **Good** to Make Some **Clever** Points Too*

Starting with an obvious point often makes it easier to think of more subtle ones, like this.

> *Jerry really doesn't want fried artichokes for breakfast — he'd "much rather" have toast. But despite that, he is very polite to his wife. All he says is that he'd be "quite happy" with toast. This shows how kind he is. He doesn't want to hurt her feelings.*

Notice how it links closely to the story and uses two quotes. It also explains what this tells us about Jerry.

It's all about getting a balance

You need to have plenty of points to make in your mini-essay, but they don't all have to be ground-breaking. As long as you go on to expand on each point, you'll be fine. If you can come up with the odd clever point though, you'll really impress the examiner.

Mini-Essay Questions

Here are a few more specific examples of things to look for when you're writing a mini-essay.

Pay Attention to the Writer's **Choice** of **Words**

This question asks you "how does the writer describe...". That makes it especially important to look at what words the writer has chosen to use. One single word can tell you a lot.

Jerry's wife annoys him but he doesn't let it show. He only groans "inwardly" rather than doing it out loud. That shows he's considerate.

Here's a good example of how one word can tell you something important about a character.

The writer says that Jerry smiles "patiently". That shows that Jerry is patient with his wife even though she annoys him.

The writer doesn't use the word "patiently" by chance. He/she wants to show us that Jerry is generally a patient kind of guy.

He calls her "love" twice. This shows how affectionate he is.

Not so obvious, this. Remember that the words people use can be really important.

Make some clever points now and again

Sometimes the important bits just leap right out at you — remember, nothing is too obvious to mention, as long as you explain your points. Keep looking for the more subtle things though.

Mini-Essay Questions

It's really important that you follow the pointers in mini-essay questions.

Tackle the Pointers **One At A Time**

Pointer number two (see p35) is "how he responds to his workplace".

So, we're just looking for descriptions of how Jerry reacts to the workplace itself.

Bit from the story:

> He positively bounced and skipped the ten minute walk to his shop, so full of energy was he feeling.

You could write this:

> *Jerry is very keen to get to work — he "positively bounced and skipped". This shows how much he likes going to work.*

Bit from the story:

> The door to Jerry's bakery was open, and he could smell the sweet aroma of freshly baking bread. He filled his lungs and beamed with pride...

You could write this:

> *Jerry "beamed with pride" when he gets to his shop. This shows how proud and happy he is with the shop's success.*

Bit from the story:

> As he closed the factory door behind him and surveyed the dozens of workers ... finally, he reflected, all those years of enterprise and hard work had paid off.

You could write this:

> *Looking at his factory, Jerry thinks about how "all those years of enterprise and hard work had paid off". He's pleased with his achievements.*

Mini-Essay Questions

This page gives you a couple more great tips for mini-essays.

*You Can Give **Mini-Overviews** for the Pointers*

It's a good idea to give a short overview for each individual pointer. You could start answering the next pointer ("the way he treats his employees") like this:

Jerry's state of mind is also revealed by the considerate way in which he treats his employees.

Writing a linking sentence like this is a clever trick. It proves that you're carefully following the question.

Then you can go on to make specific points about Jerry and his employees.

*Just **Write** Things Down As You **Find** Them*

Now you can move smoothly on to the third pointer: "the way he treats his employees".

Read the text again looking for bits about Jerry and his employees. When you find a bit that's relevant to the question, simply write it down and say what it shows.

1. *It says that Jerry had given Wayne "a big pay rise". This shows Jerry is generous and wants to share his success.*

2. *The writer describes Jerry as smiling "benevolently" when he's talking to Lisa. This word means he's full of goodwill.*

3. *Jerry praises his employees. He tells Wayne the bread "smells wonderful", and he says to Lisa "keep up the good work". He's in a good mood and he's pleased with what his workers are doing.*

Keep quoting from the story and explaining why the quotes are relevant.

All these tips will make your life easier

It might look like there's loads to remember for these questions, but keep going. Once you've done a few practice questions, it'll start feeling a lot more natural. And the more of these tips you put into practice, the more confident you'll feel in the exam.

Mini-Essay Questions

One last page on mini-essays — if you know all the stuff from these last six pages, you should have nothing to worry about when it comes to doing one of these questions for real in the exam.

There's **No Such Thing** As Being **Too Obvious**

Nearly there — just the last pointer to cover. Now we're looking for examples of what Jerry's reactions to his customers tell us about his state of mind.

I've said it before and I'll say it again — don't be scared to state the obvious.

Every day he saw customers' smiling faces in his shop, and it always gave him a warm glow of satisfaction.

Jerry is pleased that his shop is making other people happy — it gives him "a warm glow of satisfaction".

Look at the words the writer has chosen. They can tell you a lot.

By giving the old woman a free bun, Jerry again shows his kind and generous state of mind.

The writer uses the word "considerate" when Jerry puts his arm round the old woman. This shows he's caring.

Use all the hints you're given

Don't make things more difficult than they need to be. Always read the handy pointers you get underneath the question — and any other clues you get from the wording of the question — and use them when you go about your answer.

Warm-up and Worked Exam Questions

These warm-up questions will remind you of some helpful tactics for tackling the Reading Paper.

Warm-up Questions

1) What's the best way to prove to the examiners that you've got your answers from the text and not just had a guess at them?
2) Picture this scene: "Charlie opened the present with a sneer."
What does the word "sneer" tell us about Charlie's reaction to the present?
3) Put these activities in the order they should happen in the exam:
a) Write down your answer. b) Find the paragraph the question tells you to look at.
c) Read the question. d) Re-read the paragraph and decide what to write.

Worked Exam Question

This paragraph is from a brochure by Exodus, advertising biking holidays abroad.

> One of Europe's most exciting, yet least known, mountain biking areas lies deep in southern France. Full of technical trails and rocky single-tracks, the limestone region of Roquefort, just west of the Cevennes National Park, is a mountain-biker's playground. Cutting through the plateaux are the steep gorges of the Tarn, with their challenging climbs and descents, and in the eastern part of the region fast trails sweep through the cool chestnut and oak woodlands of the Cevennes. It's the perfect area for fit and experienced bikers looking for a workout.

1. Write down a word from the first sentence which sums up the impression the writer wants you to get of the trip.

exciting

(1 mark)

2. In the third sentence, two contrasting pieces of landscape are mentioned. What are they?

"Steep gorges" and "cool chestnut and oak woodlands".

(2 marks)

This is all you have to put for 2 marks. They don't ask you to comment or explain.

3. How does the brochure try to make the holiday sound appealing to mountain bikers?

Start by using the wording in the question, then use the text to answer the question. This is a 'how' question so it's vital that you explain the effects of the phrases you quote.

The brochure makes the holiday sound appealing by calling it "a mountain biker's playground". This gives us a sense that it would be fun for someone who enjoys mountain biking. It also says that some of the climbs are "challenging" and "fast" which fits the idea of an energetic and active holiday for an expert. The word "perfect" helps them to sum up all the details they've given so far.

(3 marks)

This may seem obvious but it's something the writer's done on purpose. And you've spotted it.

Worked Exam Questions

Here are some more worked exam questions. They show you how you can use all this advice to write good exam answers. Have a good look, because there's a double helping of exam questions for you to have a go at yourself on pages 44-47.

Worked Exam Questions

This is the beginning of a story by Paul Jennings called *Spaghetti Pig-Out*.

> Guts Garvey was a real mean kid. He made my life miserable. I don't know why he didn't like me. I hadn't done anything to him. Not a thing.
>
> He wouldn't let any of the other kids hang around with me. I was on my own. Anyone in the school who spoke to me was in his bad books. I wandered around the yard at lunch time like a dead leaf blown in the wind.
>
> I tried everything. I even gave him my pocket money one week. He just bought a block of chocolate from the canteen and ate it in front of me. Without even giving me a bit. What a rat.
>
> After school I had only one friend. My cat — Bad Smell. She was called that because now and then she would make a bad smell. Well, she couldn't help it. Everyone has their faults. She was a terrific cat. But still. A cat is not enough. You need other kids for friends too.

1. What does the first paragraph tell us about the narrator's thoughts on Guts Garvey?

   The narrator thinks that Guts Garvey is really mean for picking on him.

   He also doesn't understand why Guts does it.

   (2 marks)

2. a) Which simile in the second paragraph describes how lonely the narrator was?

   "I wandered around the yard at lunch time like a dead leaf blown in the wind."

   (1 mark)

   b) Explain why this phrase is effective.

   A leaf being blown by the wind is drifting around with no real place to go, just like the narrator.

   (2 marks)

3. Explain how the tone changes slightly in the last paragraph.

   In the first three paragraphs the tone is quite sad because the narrator is telling us how miserable and lonely he is. In the fourth paragraph he introduces a touch of comedy by talking about his cat who makes bad smells.

   (2 marks)

They'll give you two marks for this if you write about the sadness of the first bit and the comedy in the second bit. They want to see that you've spotted the contrast.

Worked Exam Questions

Worked Exam Questions

In this extract, the writer begins to describe what it might be like to be attacked by piranhas.

Swim with the fishes *by Greg Emmanuel*

These are no ordinary fish. Although piranhas aren't much larger than a good-sized goldfish, they have the dentition* to clear the flesh off any animal's bones — including yours. A piranha can go from open mouth to clenched teeth in less than five milliseconds — that's less time than it takes you to blink. Their jaws have an interlocking design: the top triangular teeth fit snugly into the gaps between the bottom teeth, snapping shut like a steel trap. And each individual tooth is as sharp as a razor blade.

Piranhas also have excellent senses: good vision, a well developed sense of smell, and a system of pores along their body that allows them to detect distant disturbances in the water. When your splashing feet enter their territory, the nearest piranha is thirty yards away — but can cover that distance in a few seconds. As you wrestle with your canoe, pushing and pulling it over the sandbank, you suddenly feel an unspeakable pain and yank your left foot out of the water.

*dentition = teeth

1. What shape are the piranhas' top teeth?

   They are triangular.

   (1 mark)

Look at the difference in length between the one mark answer and the five mark answer.

2. How does the writer build up a sense of how dangerous the piranha fish is?
   In your answer you should write about:
   - the way he starts the first paragraph
   - the physical details he gives about the piranhas
   - the language he uses to describe their teeth

   The writer creates a sense of how dangerous the piranha is by first warning that they are not "ordinary fish". He compares their size to a harmless goldfish but then he says that, unlike goldfish, their teeth can strip the flesh off any animal. When he adds "even yours" it makes us feel directly threatened.

   He gives alarming physical details about their teeth: he says they can clench in "less than five milliseconds". He also says they have excellent vision, smell and movement detectors, which emphasises the danger. He says each tooth is "as sharp as a razor blade", showing how easily they could cut through flesh. Another effective comparison is when he describes jaws "snapping shut like a steel trap". This gives us a strong sense of how fast they could bite.

   (5 marks)

Exam Questions

Now you've seen how it's done, I'm sure you're just itching to have a go at some Reading Paper questions yourself. Well all right then — read the text on this page and have a go at the questions on the next one. Then do the same for the ones on pages 46-47 (have a lie down in between if you like). I know it's a pain, but if you get plenty of practice in now, the real exam will be miles easier.

Exam Questions

In this extract from the novel *The Picture of Dorian Gray* by Oscar Wilde, Hallward has just finished painting the picture of Dorian.

Dorian...passed listlessly in front of his picture and turned towards it. When he saw it he drew back, and his cheeks flushed for a moment with pleasure. A look of joy came into his eyes, as if he had recognized himself for the first time. He stood there motionless, and in wonder, dimly conscious that Hallward was speaking to him, but not catching the meaning of his words. The sense of his own beauty came on him like a revelation. He had never felt it before. Basil Hallward's compliments had seemed to him to be merely the charming exaggerations of friendship. He had listened to them, laughed at them, forgotten them. They had not influenced his nature. Then had come Lord Henry, with his strange panegyric* on youth, his terrible warning of its brevity. That had stirred him at the time, and now, as he stood gazing at the shadow of his own loveliness, the full reality of the description flashed across him. Yes, there would be a day when his face would be wrinkled and wizen, his eyes dim and colourless, the grace of his figure broken and deformed. The scarlet would pass away from his lips, and the gold steal from his hair. The life that was to make his soul would mar his body. He would become ignoble, hideous, and uncouth.

As he thought of it, a sharp pang of pain struck like a knife across him, and made each delicate fibre of his nature quiver. His eyes deepened into amethyst*, and a mist of tears came across them.

He felt as if a hand of ice had been laid upon his heart.

"Don't you like it?" cried Hallward at last, stung a little by the lad's silence, and not understanding what it meant.

"Of course he likes it," said Lord Henry. "Who wouldn't like it? It is one of the greatest things in modern art. I will give you anything you like to ask for it. I must have it."

"It is not my property, Harry."

"Whose property is it?"

"Dorian's, of course."

"He is a very lucky fellow."

"How sad it is!" murmured Dorian Gray, with his eyes still fixed upon his own portrait. "How sad it is! I shall grow old, and horrid, and dreadful. But this picture will remain always young. It will never be older than this particular day of June. . . . If it was only the other way! If it was I who were to be always young, and the picture that were to grow old! For this—for this—I would give everything! Yes, there is nothing in the whole world I would not give!"

*panegyric = a speech in praise of something
*amethyst = a purple gemstone

Exam Questions

Exam Questions

1. What expression from the first sentence shows that Dorian is feeling anxious?

   ....

   (1 mark)

2. Why did Dorian think Hallward's compliments about his looks were not genuine?

   ....

   ....

   (1 mark)

3. Why does Hallward think that Dorian might not like the picture?

   ....

   (1 mark)

4. Pick out **two** expressions that suggest that Dorian is vulnerable and sensitive.

   ....

   ....

   (2 marks)

5. How do we know that Dorian is becoming obsessed with his own appearance?
   In your answer you should write about:
   - his reaction to the picture
   - his thoughts about getting older
   - what he says in the final paragraph

   ....

   ....

   ....

   ....

   ....

   ....

   ....

   ....

   ....

   ....

   (5 marks)

Exam Questions

Exam Questions

This piece of writing is taken from the website of an environmental organisation called Greenpeace. It is aimed at young people and tries to get them involved in a campaign against the destruction of ancient forests all over the world.

Kids For Forests

Young people all over the world are standing up for our planet's last ancient forests, and you can too.

There are seven big intact ancient forests. We need to put these "treasure chests of the Earth" under full protection.

Over 80 percent of the ancient forests originally in existence have already been destroyed. Giant trees from the Amazon end up as plywood boards and trees thousands of years old are boiled down to pulp, just to make everyday products.

Kids and young people all over the world are saying "NO" to ancient forest destruction, and together with Greenpeace have launched Kids for Forests. The project is currently active in more than 15 different countries in Europe, Asia, North America and South America where young people are standing up for the protection of the Earth's last ancient forests.

And, by the way, this is not the first time that Kids for Forests all over the world have stood up for the protection of the ancient forests. In 2001 and 2002, more than 35,000 kids and young people were fighting to save ancient forests all over the world. More than 1,000 came to the Ancient Forest summit in The Hague, Netherlands — an important international UN conference. They handed over petitions signed by more than 240,000 people, and called on politicians to take action at last. "Stop talking!" was their message. "Act now!"

The politicians promised to stop the die-off of species worldwide by 2010 — but they still haven't even begun. Fortunately however, environmentalists all over the world — including Kids for Forests — are seeing to it that, bit by bit, ancient forests are being saved.

In other words, it's high time that we reminded politicians what their job is. Soon we have an ideal chance to do that: the international conference in Kuala Lumpur, Malaysia, the Convention on Biological Diversity in February 2004. Kids for Forests is starting up a worldwide protest to remind politicians of their promises and responsibilities as "keepers of the forest treasures".

The Kids for Forests have fought like tigers for the last two years and will show their claws again and say: "Stop talking! Act now!"

You can help too! You can become an Ancient Forest Ambassador.

Exam Questions

Exam Questions

1. How many big ancient forests are there left which are still in one piece?

....

(1 mark)

2. Look at paragraphs 5 and 8 then write down the words you think make up the Kids for Forests slogan.

....

(1 mark)

3. a) What does paragraph 3 tell us that ancient trees are being used for?

....

(1 mark)

b) What does the writer want us to think about this use?

....

(1 mark)

4. What does the writer imply about politicians in paragraph 7?

....

....

(2 marks)

5. How does the writer try to persuade young people to become involved in the campaign? In your answer you should write about:

- the first and last paragraphs
- the use of dates and statistics
- the writer's choice of language

....

....

....

....

....

....

....

....

....

(5 marks)

Revision Summary Questions

Revision Summary questions... not the most exciting things, but they ARE really useful. You can really test your knowledge and make sure you know it all. If there's anything you get stuck on, then go straight back over those pages, and learn it. Reading test success is all about how you tackle the questions. Pretty obvious really, but that's why this section is so important.

1) How do you find the answers to short questions?
   a) Look in the paragraph they tell you to look in.
   b) Quickly read through the whole text again.
   c) You have to remember them from the text.
2) What type of question do you need to pick out individual words for?
3) Writing obvious points in your Reading answers will do two of these things. Which ones?
   a) Lose you marks.
   b) Help you to think of cleverer points.
   c) Nothing at all.
   d) Waste time.
   e) Win you marks.
4) What's the big deal about quoting?
5) How can you start your answers?
6) How can you back up your points?
7) When the question has handy pointers underneath, how many of them should you write about?
8) 90% of Columbian fruit bats think that authors just throw words together at random. Are they right? If not, what should your approach to it be?
9) Is it better to talk about the pointers:
   a) kind of mixed in together,
   b) just one at a time,
   c) in Latin?
   Why?

Give Reasons

This is a bargain basement of a section — it'll really help your marks on the Reading Paper and the Shakespeare Paper. That's excellent value.

You Have to Give **Examples** From the **Passage You've Read**

You have to give reasons for what you say — examples from the passage you've read that show where your answer comes from.

If you don't give reasons, the examiners can't tell if you know what you're talking about. Examples show you haven't got it right by a lucky fluke.

The women at the banjo club aren't very friendly. In fact they're downright rude.

This answer doesn't give any reasons.

The women at the banjo club aren't very friendly — they ignore Mrs Icenoggle when she tries to say hello.

In fact they're downright rude — they look at her, but then they start talking among themselves.

This answer gives a reason from the writing to justify every point it makes. That's loads better.

Every Time You Make a **Point** — Give an **Example**

It's easy to forget to give examples from the bit of writing you've read. You'd think because the examiner knows what you've read, they'd easily get what you're talking about. But that's the road to losing loads of marks.

They want you to refer to the writing — as if they didn't know it. Drum this simple rule into your head:

> Every time you make a point, back it up with an example.

Never forget to back your points up

The sure-fire way to get good marks in these English SATs is to make sure you put loads of examples in your answer. Reasons and examples — nothing else is going to do.

Using Your Own Words

When you link your answer to the piece you've read, use new words to show you understand it.

Don't *Just* ***Copy*** *Bits Out*

When you give your answer, don't just copy out what the piece says word for word.
Any old fool can do that, so it doesn't prove to the examiner that you've understood it.

Here's part of a story:

"Hello," Mrs Icenoggle began to say. But the sour-faced woman turned away and started to talk to her companions.

When Mrs Icenoggle began to say hello, the sour-faced woman turned away and started to talk to her companions.

This isn't a good way to talk about the story. It uses all the same words as the story — so it doesn't show that you understand.

Put your Reason in Your ***Own Words***

Prove you've understood what you've read — use your own words.

The woman ignored Mrs Icenoggle when she tried to say hello.

All I've done here is say what happened in my own words — but it proves I know what's going on.

Be careful you don't get confused between referring to a story and quoting from it.

Quoting means copying bits out word for word and putting speech marks round them.
There's more on quoting on the next page.

Remember — when you're giving a reason, always use your own words.

You have to show you understand the story

You know you have to give reasons and explanations in your answer and that means you've got to use your own words. So kick-start your brain and say it your way — don't just copy it.

How to Quote

You can make plenty of good points in your answer, but you won't get all the marks if you don't stick in loads of lovely quotes too.

Quote, Quote, Quote — and Quote Some More

Examiners love you to quote bits from the writing. It'll get you masses of extra marks.

Quotes are great because they show exactly which bit you've got your answer from.

Quoting isn't the same as stealing words from the story or article you've read. There's a massive difference...

Quotes Have Speech Marks

Speech marks make all the difference. They show that you're quoting, not just stealing words. Without speech marks you'll lose marks.

Everything inside the speech marks is a quote. It has to be word for word what the text says.

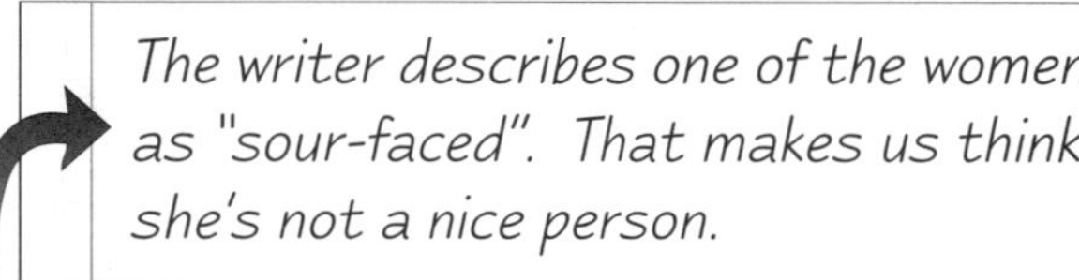
The writer describes one of the women as "sour-faced". That makes us think she's not a nice person.

Speech marks

> "Hello," Mrs Icenoggle began to say. But the sour-faced woman turned away and started to talk to her companions.
> "Did you go to Iona's party last weekend?" she asked.
> All the other women glanced briefly at Mrs Icenoggle. "I certainly did," replied one of them, "and I don't like the way Iona has redecorated her toilet."
> Mrs Icenoggle, who had no idea who Iona was, stood helplessly by the doorway...

The speech marks show that you're quoting. When you quote, make sure it's copied word for word.

The women at the banjo club are rude. They talk among themselves even though they all know Mrs Icenoggle is there — "All the other women glanced briefly at Mrs Icenoggle".

Speech marks

Quote early and quote often

Remember — copying = bad, but quoting = good (sounds daft, I know, but it's true). If you only learn one other thing about quoting, learn this: quotes always have to have speech marks.

Explain the Quote

It's no good just sticking a quote down on its own. That doesn't prove anything. You have to make sure you explain why you're using a quote.

You can Put the Explanation Before the Quote

Here I've used a quote to back up a reason I've just given.

The women at the banjo club are rude. They talk among themselves even though they all know Mrs Icenoggle is there — "All the other women glanced briefly at Mrs Icenoggle".

The answer makes a point — it says the women are rude.

Then there's a reason to back it up — the women talk among themselves even though they know Mrs Icenoggle is there.

Now there's a quote from the text. The quote proves the point that the other women all know Mrs Icenoggle is there.

You can Give the Quote First

This is an example of the second kind of way to use a quote.

The writer describes one of the women as "sour-faced". That makes us think she's not a nice person.

This time the quote gets in there first.

Then the answer explains why it's relevant to answering the question.

The writer describes one of the women as "sour-faced".

If I just wrote this bit, I wouldn't get as many marks. The examiner needs to know why you think the quote is important.

Always explain why the quote is relevant.

It doesn't matter what order you do it in — make a point, then back it up with a quote — or quote then explain. The important thing is that you always explain why your quote helps you answer the question.

Explain your quotes and your marks will shoot up

You know why you've chosen your quote. The examiners won't know — you need to tell them.

Keeping Quotes Short

Don't think that you'll get better marks for using longer quotes.
You won't. In fact you'll lose marks for it.

Never Quote More than A Few Words...

Quotes are to show that you've read the bit of text you're talking about.
You usually only need to quote a few words.

Buckingham accepts that he is getting what he deserves —
"This, this All Soul's Day to my fearful soul
Is the determined respite of my wrongs:
That high All-seer which I dallied with
Hath turned my feigned prayer on my head
And given in earnest what I begged in jest."
(Act 5, Scene 1, 18-22)

This quote is far too long. It doesn't make the answer better, and it uses up precious time that you could spend writing something else.

Buckingham accepts that he is getting what he deserves —
"This, this All Souls' Day to my fearful soul
Is the determined respite of my wrongs"
(Act 5, Scene 1, 18-19)

This quote is much better. It's short and it has everything you need to make your point.

Try to quote using as few words as possible.
Just quote a single word if it's enough to make your point.

... But Do It Often

Your answer should be full of short quotes backing up your points.

Every time you make a point, try to find a quote to back it up.

You should always try to find a relevant quote. Your answers will be much better with loads of good quotes.

Quotes should be as short as possible

You don't need to quote vast chunks of text — just the bit that makes the point. Be economical.

Warm-up and Worked Exam Questions

Time for a recap and some practice on quoting.

Warm-up Questions

1) Which of the following should you include when you make a point in your answer?
   reasons **examples** **quotes** **bribes** **explanations**
2) When you copy words out exactly as they appear in the text, what can you use to show that you haven't just stolen them?
3) A good Reading answer includes a point, an example or quote, and an explanation. Which order should they go in? (Hint: Don't rush this one.)
4) What good advice could you give someone about how much to quote?

Worked Exam Questions

The Listeners *by Walter de la Mare*

'Is there anybody there?' said the Traveller,
Knocking on the moonlit door;
And his horse in the silence champed the grasses
Of the forest's ferny floor:
And a bird flew up out of the turret,
Above the traveller's head:
And he smote upon the door again a second time;
'Is there anybody there?' he said.

1. What impression do you get of the place the Traveller has come to?

The place seems quite lonely. We are told that it is in the forest and that there is silence. A bird flies out of a "turret" which is a kind of tower and it is "above the Traveller's head" so it must be quite high. This makes the place sound like a large, old building. It might be derelict if there was a bird inside it.

(3 marks)

Explain the quote — and don't be afraid to state the obvious.

2. What have we learned about the Traveller?

Keep it simple — say what the names tell you if it's relevant.

Calling the main character "the Traveller" makes him mysterious because we are not told his name and we don't know where or why he is travelling. He also seems determined to get an answer. The word "smote" means that he banged loudly and forcefully on the door. He doesn't give up when nobody answers, and he repeats his question, "Is there anybody there?"

(3 marks)

You can work out the meaning of tricky words from the text.

Worked Exam Questions

These questions focus on language. The answers show you how to use the text to back up your points.

Worked Exam Questions

This extract is the introduction from a non-fiction book aimed at teenagers.
It is a handbook for people who want to be vegetarians.

> It all starts here — with the ultimate guide to going, being and staying veggie.
>
> This book will take you through the change from being a meatie to being a vegetarian — every step of the way. Every question answered, every doubt knocked on the head and every concern sorted.
>
> If you're already a veggie, this book will give you the confidence and knowledge to argue for your beliefs. If your parents are worried, it will put their minds at rest. If you're short of facts, you'll find them here.
>
> Farming has become a secret industry where animals are crammed together behind closed doors, away from prying eyes. Section 1 of this book shines a spotlight into the darkest corners and reveals what it's really like.

1. How does the way the first sentence is written encourage the reader to think that the book will be useful?

The writer makes a confident statement — "It all starts here". This suggests that nothing we have seen before will have been as useful. The word "ultimate" is a strong description. It supports the idea that this book is the best so far.

(2 marks)

Explain why the adjectives are effective.

2. Explain how the writer's language suggests that the farming industry has something to hide, and how this idea is important to the handbook's message.

Find the words and phrases that relate to the question and explain why they're effective.

The writer starts by calling farming a "secret industry" as if it is keeping things from the public. The phrase "behind closed doors" makes us feel things are being hidden from us. The word "crammed" makes it sound like the animals are being squeezed into as small a space as possible. The writer then hints that this book will break into this secret world. It claims to "shine a spotlight into the darkest corner". This means the book will discuss areas of farming which are usually ignored. It sounds as though all the sinister details will be investigated and shown up.

(4 marks)

Exam Questions

Here's another chance to put all this advice into practice.
Have a go at these exam questions, and try to use all the tips you've learned so far.

Exam Questions

In this extract from *Harry Potter and the Goblet of Fire* by J. K. Rowling, Frank, the gardener, has been hiding outside a room in the house where he works, listening to a conversation inside. He is very frightened.

And then Frank heard movement behind him in the dark passageway. He turned to look behind him, and found himself paralysed with fright.

Something was slithering towards him along the dark corridor floor, and as it drew nearer to the sliver of firelight, he realised with a thrill of terror that it was a gigantic snake, at least twelve feet long. Horrified, transfixed, Frank stared at it as its undulating body cut a wide, curving track through the thick dust on the floor, coming closer and closer — what was he to do? The only means of escape was into the room where the two men sat plotting murder, yet if he stayed where he was the snake would surely kill him —

But before he had made his decision, the snake was level with him, and then, incredibly, miraculously, it was passing; it was following the spitting, hissing noises made by the cold voice beyond the door, and in seconds, the tip of its diamond patterned tail had vanished through the gap.

There was sweat on Frank's forehead now, and the hand on the walking stick was trembling.

1. What impression do you get of the house where the story takes place?

....

....

(2 marks)

2. What is Frank's reaction when the snake slithers past him?

....

....

(2 marks)

3. How does the writer make Frank's fear obvious to us all the way through the extract?

(5 marks)

(You'll need to use a separate sheet of paper to answer this question.)

Revision Summary Questions

This is a pretty short section, but don't think you can skip through it really quickly. Quoting is really important — there's no way to get all the marks you want without a clear and thorough understanding of the whole of this section. There are good and bad ways of quoting, and you have to get it right. Just bunging loads of random quotes in all over the place won't do you any favours at all. Test yourself on these questions, and go over the section until you can do them all.

1) What do you have to do to back up every point you make?
2) When you give your answer, is it OK to write your reasons in exactly the same words as the piece of writing uses?
3) If it's not OK, why not? What should you do instead?
4) When can you copy the words exactly?
5) How do you show that something's a quote?
6) Is using quotes:
   a) a bad idea
   b) a good idea, but only if there's time
   c) a great idea?
7) What are the two important ways of giving a reason and explaining it with a quote?
8) What are the rules on how long a quote should be?
9) How often should you use quotes?

What You Have To Do

On the Shakespeare paper you have to answer a question about the set scenes you're doing. This section is full of tips on how to answer the Shakespeare question well. So get stuck in. There are two big things you have to do to get marks.

1) Show You Understand *What's Going On*

Don't worry — it's not just you who reads Shakespeare and thinks "what does it mean?"

The examiners know that — and you'll get plenty of marks just for showing that you know what's happening.

To show you understand the set scenes, you might need to:

1) Write about the way the characters are feeling.
2) Write about Shakespeare's choice of words.
3) Write about some of the ideas and themes.
4) Write some ideas about how the scenes should be acted.

2) Use **Quotes** To Back Up Your Points

We've already talked about how important quoting is in your reading paper. It's just as important in the Shakespeare Paper — if not more so. You have to quote.

If you talk about the play without using bags of quotes, and explaining why your quotes are important, they won't be convinced that you really know your stuff.

Make sure you stick your quotes in speech marks, and only use the exact words that Shakespeare uses.

Plus You'll Do Better if You **Write Well**

1) You don't have to use loads of posh, long words on the set scenes question. But if you write badly the examiners won't be able to understand what you're saying, and that'll make them grumpy and stingy with marks.

2) Don't forget to write in paragraphs. Every time you want to talk about a new idea, start a new paragraph.

3) Here's the tough one — try to sound interested in the play, even if you don't like it. Show the examiners that you're keen by using lots of interesting words and phrases in your answer.

Shakespeare questions don't have to be really difficult

Your three tips for Shakespeare success — show you get what's going on, use plenty of quotes from the play, and write clearly in proper paragraphs, with some interesting words.

Shakespeare's Language

It doesn't matter if you think Shakespeare is weird or boring. The important thing is it's not impossible. This section's here to make it all less scary and more straightforward.

It's **Weird** — but it gets **Easier** With Practice

Once you get used to the unusual language, Shakespeare is much simpler. Remember, you don't have to like it, but you do have to do an exam on it.

Shakespeare can be really exciting. The plays have stories full of violence, villains, murder, love, double-crossing and betrayal.

The key thing about Shakespeare is getting to grips with the strange language. It's not easy, but you can learn how to do it. Practise reading your set scenes — the more you read them, the easier they'll be to understand.

You **Don't** Have To Understand **Every Word**

That's right — if you read it loads and there are still bits you don't understand, don't worry. As long as you've got the idea of what's going on, you'll be fine.

Take a look at this — it's the kind of question you'll get in the exam.

How important is the use of magic in Prospero's plans?

This tests if you've understood what Prospero is trying to do, and how he uses magic to do it. If you show you understand basically what's going on, you don't need to explain the meaning of every single word.

Don't look at your exam paper and start panicking just because there's a tiny bit of the scene you don't understand.

You don't need to understand every single word.
You just need to understand what's going on and be able to pick out some good quotes.

Don't let the language put you off

Shakespeare isn't that boring if you understand the weird language. It gets easier with practice, and in any case you don't have to understand all of it — as long as you get the basic idea.

Tricky Play Terms

You just have to learn these words. Without them, the play will never quite make sense.

A Play is Divided into **Acts** and **Scenes**

The play is divided into five big sections, called acts. Each act is like an episode of a TV serial — lots of things happen in it, but it's only part of the whole thing.

Each act is made up of smaller sections called scenes. Scenes are just a way of breaking up the story. A new scene starts when time has passed or the story moves to a different place.

'Act' and 'Scene' are two words you're likely to have to use a lot in the SAT, so make sure you know what they mean.

In the exam, you'll probably get a question on two extracts from different scenes.

Shakespeare Wrote **Three Kinds of Play**

Shakespeare wrote three main kinds of play. You can impress the examiner by using these words in your SAT, so make sure you know what they mean.

TRAGEDIES — People die at the end.

Romeo and Juliet and *Macbeth* are tragedies.

COMEDIES — People get married at the end.

The Tempest and *Much Ado About Nothing* are comedies.

HISTORIES — These are based on real history.

Richard III and *Henry V* are histories.

Characters are the **People** in the Play

There are a few main characters in each play that you have to know all about. There are also loads of minor characters who don't do anything very important.

For example, in *Richard III*, Richard, Buckingham and Queen Elizabeth are important characters.

Make sure you know what's what

Don't get acts and scenes mixed up, and remember those three types of play. You'll be able to impress the examiner with them, and that means a better grade.

More Play Features

A lot of the things you'll find odd when you read a scene from Shakespeare are there because it's a play. Learn what it all means now and you won't be confused in the exam.

*Plays are Written to be **Acted***

1) There's a massive difference between a Shakespeare play and a novel or short story. A novel tells a story by describing it to you. A play tells a story by showing it to you.

2) You don't get any long describing bits in a play. The actors show the audience what's going on by the way they say their lines — laughing, shouting or whatever — as well as what they say.

3) The audience don't have the playscript in front of them, so the actors have to do all the work.

4) In the exam, you have to do all the work. You have to work out what's going on just by reading the scenes.

*You have to **Imagine** the Script Being **Acted***

When you read the play, it's hard to imagine what it would look like on stage. Try to see the characters in your mind. Think about:

- what kind of people they are
- how you think they would say their lines
- how they would act

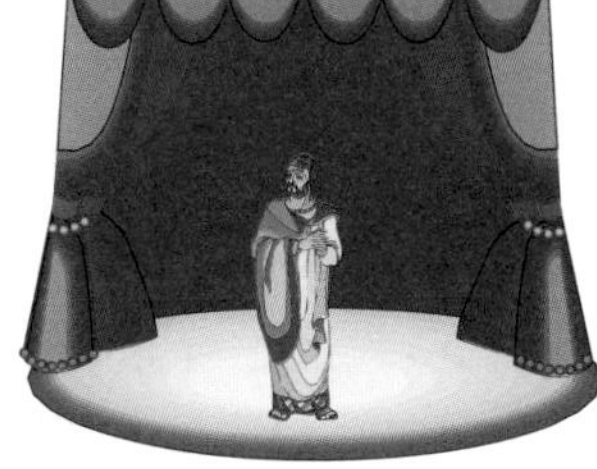

If you want some idea of how the play might look when it's acted out, you could watch it on video or DVD. Your school might have a copy of it — it's worth asking. Just remember: each version will be different.

It's really important that you think about how the play would look and sound when it's acted on a stage — because that's what Shakespeare was thinking about when he wrote it.

Try to think about how the play would look on stage

Plays were written to be acted out on a stage, so having to read them can feel a bit odd. But there's no one to act it out in the exam — so you have to understand it all from the script.

More Play Features

A lot of the things that happen in Shakespeare plays seem odd to us reading it now. This is partly because they were written about 400 years ago, but also because Shakespeare uses certain techniques to get messages across to the audience watching the play.

Sometimes Characters **Talk To Themselves**

This seems strange. People in real life don't usually talk to themselves — if they did, pretty soon you'd start to worry about them.

Characters in plays do this so the audience can hear what they're thinking and feeling. They're really talking for the benefit of the audience.

RICHARD Was ever woman in this humour woo'd?
Was ever woman in this humour won?
I'll have her, but I will not keep her long.
What, I that kill'd her husband and his father:
To take her in her heart's extremest hate,
With curses in her mouth, tears in her eyes,
The bleeding witness of her hatred by,
Having God, her conscience, and these bars against me —
And I, no friends to back my suit at all
But the plain devil and dissembling looks —
And yet to win her, all the world to nothing!

Everyone has left. Richard is on his own.

Richard's not actually talking to anyone — he's just talking to himself. This means he's showing his true feelings.

Richard is thinking these things. People don't usually think out loud, but you wouldn't know what was going on in Richard's head if he didn't tell you. Shakespeare makes him say it out loud.

If a character is talking to himself on an empty stage like this, it's called a soliloquy. Soliloquies are important because when they talk to each other, characters often lie — but here they tell you what they really think.

Sometimes Characters **Don't Want** to be **Overheard**

Sometimes characters say thoughts aloud when other characters are on the stage. When you see the word [Aside], that's what's happening — the audience can hear, but the other characters can't.

Soliloquies and asides are really important

Because Shakespeare wrote plays and not novels, he couldn't just describe what the characters were thinking, like a novelist can. That's why you get characters talking to themselves. When this happens, you know what they're saying is really important to the play.

More Play Features

When you read Shakespeare plays, it helps if you imagine what would be happening if they were being said by actors on stage. Luckily, you get some clues as to what would be going on.

Stage Directions Give a Few Clues

Stage directions show the actors what to do, when to come in and when to leave the stage.

Swoon means "faint", so this stage direction tells the person playing Hero to faint.

LEONATO Hath no man's dagger here a point for me?
[Hero swoons]
BEATRICE Why how now, cousin? Wherefore sink you down?
DON JOHN Come, let us go. These things, come thus to light,
Smother her spirits up.
[Exeunt Don Pedro, Don John and Claudio]
BENEDICK How doth the lady?
BEATRICE Dead, I think. Help, uncle!
Hero, why Hero! Uncle! Signior Benedick! Friar!
LEONATO Oh Fate, take not away thy heavy hand!
Death is the fairest cover for her shame
That may be wished for.

Exeunt is a daft word. All it means is that more than one person leaves the stage.

The character names here tell you who's speaking. So it's Leonato who's speaking these lines.

Stage directions are great, because they tell you the basics of what's happening on stage. Always read them when you read a play.

The Director Decides the Rest

Sometimes the stage directions tell the actors how to say their lines. More often though, the director has to work out how the actors should say the lines — sadly, angrily or whatever.

The director decides what the actors should do to help the audience understand what's going on. Unfortunately, you don't have a director to help you in the exam — you've got to figure it all out for yourself, from the words.

You might be asked in the SAT to imagine that you're a director, and you have to tell the actors how to act in that scene.

Don't ignore the stage directions

So that's what stage directions are, then. Use them to help you imagine how the actors would be saying the words and what they'd be doing on the stage. Don't forget: Exeunt = They exit.

Warm-up and Exam Questions

There's a lot to remember for the Shakespeare questions, but it'll be easier once you've done a few practice questions. You'll be fighting duels, crying for your horse and your mates will start calling you "my liege". Trust me.

Warm-up Questions

1) What's the best way to get to grips with the unusual Shakespearean language in your set scenes?
2) Do you need to make sure you understand every single word of your Shakespeare set scenes?
3) a) How many acts are there in a Shakespeare play?
   b) What is normally the reason for starting a new scene?
4) Did Shakespeare write his plays to be:
   a) acted out?
   b) read?
   c) used to line the rabbit's hutch?
5) How can you work out the way a character might say their lines?

These questions might not be on your particular set scenes, but they'll give you the chance to get used to the style of the Shakespeare Question. So give 'em a go and see how you get on. **Look up the scenes in a copy of the play.**

Exam Questions

1. **The Tempest**
   Act 1, Scene 2, lines 309-376
   Act 3, Scene 2, line 86 to end of scene

   These line numbers can vary depending on which version of the play you're using.

   In the first of these scenes, Caliban argues with Prospero.
   In the second of these scenes, Caliban starts a plot to kill Prospero.

   How is Caliban's character portrayed in these scenes?

   Support your ideas by referring to the extracts.

   (18 marks)

Exam Questions

Exam Questions

2. **The Tempest**
   Act 2 Scene 1, line 241 to end of scene
   Act 3 Scene 3, lines 1-35

   In these scenes we see Antonio plotting to kill Alonso and Gonzalo.

   How is Antonio presented as an evil and unpleasant character in these scenes?

   Support your ideas by referring to the extracts.

   (18 marks)

3. **The Tempest**
   Act 1, Scene 2, line 411 to end of scene
   Act 5, Scene 1, lines 120-171

   In the first of these scenes, Prospero decides to test Ferdinand's love for Miranda. In the second of these scenes, Prospero confronts the people who betrayed him.

   What impressions do you gain of Prospero's character from these two scenes and why?

   Support your ideas by referring to the extracts.

   (18 marks)

4. **The Tempest**
   Act 1, Scene 2, lines 190-305
   Act 5, Scene 1, lines 83-102

   In these extracts, Prospero talks to the spirit Ariel and gives him orders.

   What do these scenes show about the relationship between Prospero and Ariel?

   Support your ideas by referring to the extracts.

   (18 marks)

Exam Questions

Exam Questions

5. **Richard III**
   Act 3 Scene 5, lines 1-71
   Act 5 scene 4

   These line numbers can vary depending on which version of the play you're using.

   In the first of these extracts, Richard and Buckingham pretend to be under attack. In the second extract, Richard is fighting bravely.

   Explain what we learn about Richard's character from these two scenes.

   Support your ideas by referring to the extracts.

   (18 marks)

6. **Richard III**
   Act 1 Scene 4, lines 1-75
   Act 5 Scene 3, lines 119-223

   In both these extracts characters have important dreams.

   Explain how the characters react to their dreams, and how they're influenced by them.

   Support your ideas by referring to the extracts.

   (18 marks)

7. **Richard III**
   Act 1 Scene 2, lines 151-226
   Act 3 Scene 7, lines 116 to end of scene

   These two scenes show Richard acting in order to deceive people.

   Explain how Shakespeare uses language to show how good Richard is at acting a part to get his own way.

   Support your ideas by referring to the extracts.

   (18 marks)

Exam Questions

Exam Questions

8. Much Ado About Nothing
Act 2 Scene 1, lines 1-120
Act 4 Scene 1

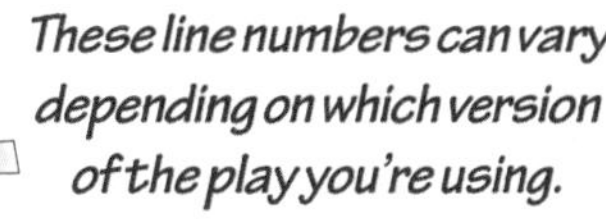

Beatrice and Hero have been brought up to be as close as sisters.
In these scenes we see them both during a happy time and a difficult time.

Explain what the scenes show us about the differences between Beatrice and Hero.

Support your ideas by referring to the extracts.

(18 marks)

9. Much Ado About Nothing
Act 2 Scene 1, lines 1-114
Act 5 Scene 1, lines 1-85

In both these scenes we see Leonato and Antonio at home together, but the atmosphere in the two scenes is very different.

Explain how Shakespeare creates the atmosphere in each scene.

Support your ideas by referring to the extracts.

(18 marks)

10. Much Ado About Nothing
Act 1 Scene 1, line 85 to end of scene
Act 1 Scene 3

Although Don Pedro and Don John are brothers, their behaviour and their attitudes are very different.

Show how these two scenes emphasise the differences between Don Pedro and Don John.

Support your ideas by referring to the extracts.

(18 marks)

The Language

When you first read a Shakespeare play, it seems like you'll never understand a word. Don't give up, though. The more you read the play, the easier it gets and the more you'll get it.

The Language ***Isn't*** *Everyday* ***Modern English***

Shakespeare wasn't trying to confuse you by using funny language — believe it or not, when he was alive people really did use those strange words. He wrote his plays about 400 years ago.

See if this speech from *The Tempest* is any clearer after you've read the "translation".

Background: In the past, Alonso betrayed Prospero when Antonio robbed him of his title of Duke of Milan. Prospero was set adrift at sea. Now, after making sure that Alonso and his followers have had a horrible time, Prospero finally reveals himself and prepares to forgive them.

Here's what's in the play:

PROSPERO Behold, Sir King,
The wronged Duke of Milan, Prospero.
For more assurance that a living prince
Does now speak to thee, I embrace thy body,
And to thee and thy company I bid
A hearty welcome.
ALONSO Whe'er thou be'st he or no,
Or some enchanted trifle to abuse me,
As late I have been, I not know. Thy pulse
Beats as of flesh and blood; and since I saw thee,
Th'affliction of my mind amends, with which
I fear a madness held me.

This is roughly what it means:

"Look, it's me, Prospero, the bloke who was robbed of being Duke of Milan. To prove it really is me, I'm going to give you a hug. A big welcome to you and your mates."

"Whether it really is you, or some weird magic trick to torture me like the others, I don't know. You've got a pulse just like a real person. And since you appeared, I've felt a lot better, and I don't feel like I'm going mad any more."

Some Sentences are in a ***Funny Order***

People swapped round the order of words a lot more in those days.
If you jiggle the word order around a bit you can usually work out what it means.

Your daughter here the princes left for dead

The princes left your daughter here for dead.

Try to pick up bits and pieces

If you don't understand it all, don't panic. Keep reading it and try to pick out the odd bit here and there. You only need to know what's going on — not every word.

The Language

Shakespeare writes a lot in verse, or poetry — and he often uses lots of words to say something simple. This page will help you to make sense of what you're reading.

Don't Stop Reading At the End of the Line

When you read verse, it's tempting to stop at the end of a line. Don't — unless there's a full stop, the sentence carries on. It makes no sense if you pause at the end of every single line. Try reading this extract from *The Tempest*.

ALONSO You cram these words into mine ears against
The stomach of my sense. Would I had never
Married my daughter there! For, coming thence,
My son is lost; and, in my rate, she too,
Who is so far from Italy removed
I ne'er again shall see her. O thou mine heir
Of Naples and of Milan, what strange fish
Hath made his meal on thee?

If you stop at the end of each line, this makes no sense. It would sound like: "O thou mine heir. Of Naples and of Milan, what strange fish. Hath made his meal on thee?"

It'll make a lot more sense if you read it all as one sentence: "Oh thou mine heir of Naples and Milan, what strange fish hath made his meal on thee?"

Don't pause at the end of lines when you're reading Shakespeare — pause when you get to punctuation, the commas and full stops, like in other writing. It'll make much more sense.

Characters Use an Awful Lot of Words

One thing you're bound to notice about Shakespeare is that the characters use an awful lot of words to say something simple.

Have another look at that speech by Alonso, from *The Tempest*. He talks for ages but all he's basically saying is this:

I'm upset because I think my son has drowned.

The way the speeches are so long-winded might be a bit irritating, but you have to know what they're about to get good marks. You have to talk about how Shakespeare uses this flowery language to show what characters are thinking and feeling.

Shakespeare's much easier if you follow the punctuation

Make sure that you don't pause at the end of each and every line — look at the punctuation instead. And bear in mind that characters use loads of words for ideas that are basically simple.

The Language

Of course, people don't walk round speaking in poetry in real life.
If you understand why Shakespeare wrote like that, you've got a head start in the exam.

Only the *Posh* Characters Talk in *Poetry*

In Shakespeare's day, writers made their posher characters talk in verse (poetry) — while the more common characters talked in normal, everyday prose (not poetry).

CLAUDIO — Sweet Hero, now thy image doth appear
In the rare semblance that I loved it first.

DOGBERRY — Come, bring away the plaintiffs. By this time our sexton hath reformed Signior Leonato of the matter. And, masters, do not forget to specify, when time and place shall serve, that I am an ass.

In this scene from *Much Ado About Nothing*, the lord Claudio talks in verse, but Dogberry (an ordinary man) talks in prose.

If Shakespeare had made Claudio talk in prose here, it would have sounded odd to audiences at the time — a bit like a BBC newsreader talking in Cockney slang.

There are *Exceptions*

Sometimes the posher characters talk in prose — like Don Pedro, Claudio and Benedick in Act V, Scene 1 of *Much Ado*. This can be confusing.

This doesn't mean they've suddenly become lower class — they're just bantering with each other in a casual, chummy way.

Also, the poorer characters sometimes talk in poetry — but usually only when they're spouting about big ideas.

The poetry is there for a reason

Shakespeare wrote in verse when a posh character was speaking, or when he wanted his writing to sound more impressive. Remember — nine times out of ten when prose crops up, it means someone common is talking.

The Language

Here's some more about poetry and the effect it creates.

Poetry Makes it Easier to Sound *Grand*

Shakespeare uses verse to make what he's writing about sound important. Here's an example:

RICHARD Now is the winter of our discontent,
Made glorious summer by this son of York,
And all the clouds that loured upon our House
In the deep bosom of the ocean buried.
Now are our brows bound with victorious wreaths,
Our bruised arms hung up for monuments,
Our stern alarums changed to merry meetings,
Our dreadful marches to delightful measures.

This is the opening of *Richard III*. Richard is talking about how the civil wars are over and a new Yorkist King has brought peace.

Rhymed Verse Sounds Even *Grander*

Shakespeare's verse doesn't always rhyme — the important thing is that the words fit a rhythm.

But sometimes Shakespeare does use rhyme to create a special effect.
He uses rhyme to sound even grander than usual.

Honour, riches, marriage blessing,
Long continuance, and increasing,
Hourly joys be still upon you!
Juno sings her blessings on you.

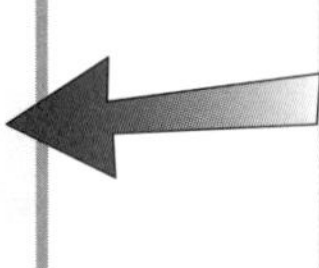

The goddesses in *The Tempest* speak in rhyme.

It makes them sound wise and knowledgeable.

Done to death by slanderous tongues
Was the Hero that here lies.
Death, in guerdon of her wrongs,
Gives her fame which never dies.

When Claudio reads the epitaph at Hero's tomb in *Much Ado About Nothing*, the rhyming creates a sad, serious mood.

You'll soon get used to the poetry

When Shakespeare makes his verses rhyme, it's very likely he's doing it to make it sound grander. And if you understand why the poetry's there, you're half way to sussing it out.

The Language

There's no denying that Shakespeare used lots of words you and I wouldn't use. Once you know what they mean, they'll cause you no trouble.

Don't Worry About the Funny **Old Words**

Don't be put off — it's normally pretty obvious what they mean.

"Thee" and "thou" both mean "you".

"Thy" means "your".

"Hath" means "has".

There are some Other **Odd** Things About the **Language**

This is partly because the English language was a bit different in Shakespeare's day. But it's also to do with Shakespeare taking a few liberties with the language so that it fits nicely into his poetry.

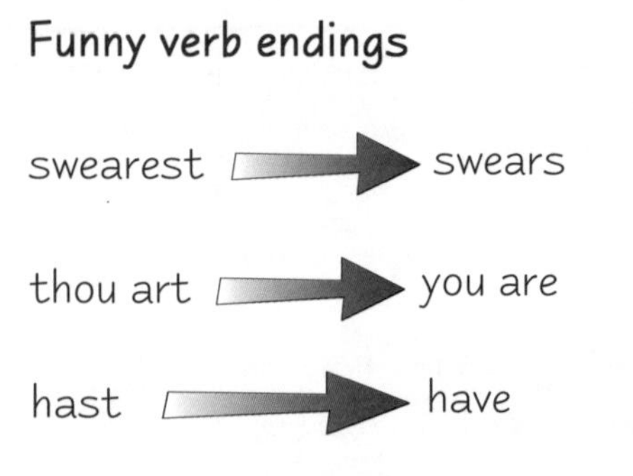

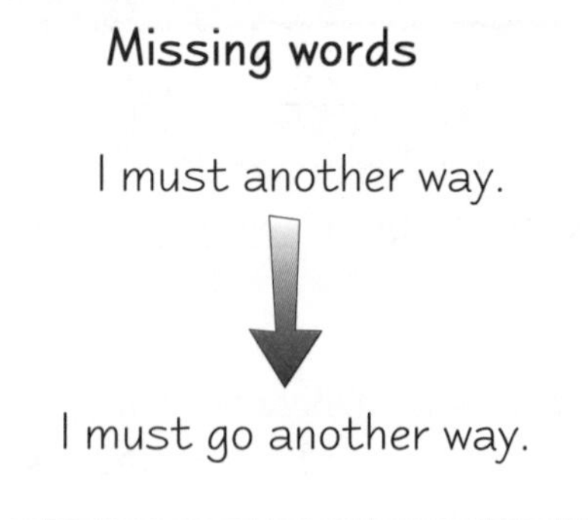

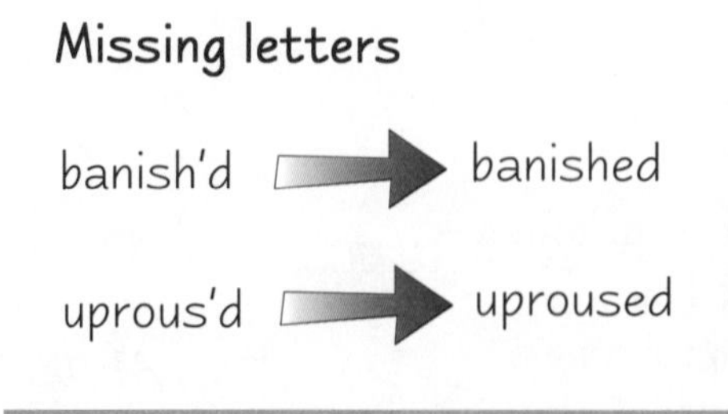

The old-fashioned language isn't that hard

The old words might seem difficult to understand, but that's only because you're not used to them. Replace them in your mind with normal ones, and it'll all make a lot more sense.

The Language

Shakespeare is always comparing things, and you'll get great marks for writing about how he does it.

You Have to Write About ***Comparisons***

Shakespeare loves comparing things to other things.
Sometimes he makes it really obvious that he's doing this.

LEONATO I pray thee cease thy counsel,
Which falls into mine ears as profitless
As water in a sieve.

The words "as ... as" show you that Shakespeare is making a comparison. Here Leonato in *Much Ado About Nothing* is saying Antonio's advice is having no effect at all.

In an exam, you would get marks for saying things like this:

> *Water passes straight through a sieve, so Leonato is saying that he simply isn't listening to Antonio's advice at all, so there's no point Antonio giving it.*

Sometimes it's a bit less obvious — and you've got to be sharp to notice he's doing it.

ANTONIO Which, of he or Adrian, for a good wager,
first begins to crow?
SEBASTIAN The old cock.
ANTONIO The cock'rel.

In this extract from *The Tempest*, Antonio and Sebastian are making fun out of Gonzalo and Adrian by comparing their conversation to cockerels crowing.

Comparisons are a key part of studying Shakespeare

Comparisons are a really major part of Shakespeare's plays. You'll be able to write about comparsions in nearly every Shakespeare question. They give you useful clues about the character who's making them — remember to talk about this in your answer.

The Language

Just a bit more on the language in Shakespeare plays. If you keep all these things in mind, you'll get to grips with the plays a lot faster.

Sometimes the Characters Seem to Speak in **Riddles**

The characters don't always mean exactly what they say — you might find this a bit annoying. But you'll get great marks if you can figure it out and explain what they do mean.

In this passage from *Much Ado About Nothing,* Don John is saying that he would rather be hated by Don Pedro than try to get him and others to like him.

DON JOHN I had rather be a canker in a hedge than a rose in his grace, and it better fits my blood to be disdained of all than to fashion a carriage to rob love from any.

A "canker" means a disease or wound — it stands for how Don John wants to annoy and embarrass his brother Don Pedro, instead of trying to find some way to "rob love" from people and get them to like him.

This is a quote from Richmond in *Richard III*.

RICHMOND The weary sun hath made a golden set
And by the bright tract of his fiery car
Gives token of a goodly day to-morrow.

All Richmond is saying here is, "looks like it'll be a nice day tomorrow".

You can get extra marks for writing about riddles

If there are riddles in the play you study, you have to be able to get your head round them. If you can explain what it means when the characters say weird things, you'll be well away.

Other Strange Things

Some of the things the characters do seem really strange to us. Remember, though, that it was all written 400 years ago — and Shakespeare chose some very odd settings.

The Character ***Names*** *Look* ***Odd***

Don't be put off by the fact that some of the characters have funny looking names. Shakespeare set some of his plays in foreign countries and gave the characters foreign names.

These are characters from *Much Ado About Nothing*.
They sound Italian because the play's set in Messina, in Italy.

Sometimes the character names are supposed to be funny. Don't worry if you don't find them side-splittingly hilarious. People's sense of humour in Shakespeare's day was different.

Life Was ***Different*** *Back Then*

Remember that things have changed a lot since Shakespeare's day — and Shakespeare set some of his plays even further back in the past than when he was writing them — which makes things seem even stranger.

1) In *The Tempest* there are magic spells and fairies who can appear in different forms. People believed in magic in Shakespeare's day more than they do now, so this wouldn't have seemed as odd to them as it does to us.

2) In *Much Ado About Nothing*, there are lots of tricks played on various characters that in real life probably no one would fall for. But this happens a lot in Shakespeare plays — you have to forget how unrealistic it may seem and just go along with it.

3) *Richard III* is about an English king who lived 500 years ago. There's loads of killing, scheming and double-crossing, which doesn't fit in with modern ideas about the royal family. But in the past royals were often involved in bloody power struggles.

Things were different back then

It's easy to get put off by how odd some of the plays seem. Remember that the world Shakespeare writes about is different from our world — then the plays will make more sense.

Warm-up and Exam Questions

Here's a chance for you to test what skills you've picked up so far regarding our friend Mr Shakespeare. We'll start with a few warm-up questions, then there's a whole load of proper exam questions to have a go at. Oh the joy.

Warm-up Questions

1) Roughly how long ago did Shakespeare write his plays?

2) When is a good time to pause if you're reading Shakespeare aloud?
   a) At the end of each line.
   b) When the bell goes.
   c) When you come to some punctuation.

3) a) Which was supposed to sound posher, talking in poetry or talking in prose?
   b) Why would Shakespeare sometimes make a common character talk in poetry?

4) Which of these are you likely to find in the language of Shakespeare's plays?

   riddles **comparisons** **rhymes**
   equations **rhythms** **some funny looking spelling**

5) Give two reasons why Shakespeare's characters might seem strange to us.

Exam Questions

1. **Much Ado About Nothing**
   Act 1 Scene 1, lines 143 to 227
   Act 5 Scene 1, lines 109 to 191

   The relationship between Claudio, Benedick and Don Pedro changes between these two scenes.

   Explain how we can tell it has changed from their conversations in each scene.

   Support your ideas by referring to the extracts.

   (18 marks)

Exam Questions

Exam Questions

2. **Much Ado About Nothing**
   Act 1 Scene 1, lines 1 to 118
   Act 5 Scene 2, line 23 to end of scene

   The relationship between Beatrice and Benedick and the way it develops is one of the important parts of the plot.

   Explain how the change in their relationship is shown by the way they speak in these two scenes.

   Support your ideas by referring to the extracts.

   (18 marks)

3. **Much Ado About Nothing**
   Act 2 Scene 3, line 87 to end of scene
   Act 3 Scene 1, line 37 to end of scene

   In these scenes, Benedick's friends trick him into believing Beatrice is in love with him. Beatrice's friends do the same to her about Benedick.

   Write about how the language in these scenes helps to create the comedy.

   Support your ideas by referring to the extracts.

   (18 marks)

4. **Much Ado About Nothing**
   Act 2 Scene 1, lines 139 to 280
   Act 4 Scene 1, lines 1 to 105

   Claudio is supposed to have the part of a typical noble lover in the play, but Don John finds him very easy to fool. He is very quick to believe that the people he cares about have betrayed him.

   Write about how these two extracts might affect an audience's impressions of Claudio.

   Support your ideas by referring to the extracts.

   (18 marks)

Exam Questions

Exam Questions

5. **Richard III**
   Act 3 Scene 1, lines 151 to end of scene
   Act 4 Scene 2

   In Act 3, Scene 1, Richard promises to make Buckingham an Earl when he becomes King. In Act 4, Scene 2, Richard has fallen out with Buckingham.

   Compare the way Richard behaves towards Buckingham in these two scenes and explain what it shows about both their characters.

   Support your ideas by referring to the extracts.

   (18 marks)

6. **Richard III**
   Act 3, Scene 4, line 58 to end of scene
   Act 4, Scene 2, lines 1 to 65

   How does Shakespeare use the language in these extracts to create an atmosphere of evil?

   Support your ideas with reference to the extracts.

   (18 marks)

7. **Richard III**
   Act 3 Scene 4
   Act 4 Scene 2

   In these two scenes we see how Richard treats people who refuse to do what he wants.

   What impression do we get of Richard's character from the way he speaks and the things he says in these two scenes?

   Support your ideas by referring to the extracts.

   (18 marks)

Exam Questions

Exam Questions

8. **The Tempest**
   Act 2, Scene 1 lines 183-295
   Act 3, Scene 2, line 87 to end of scene

   In these two scenes, characters plan to betray and kill others.

   How does Shakespeare use language to create a threatening atmosphere in these scenes?

   Support your ideas by referring to the extracts.

   (18 marks)

9. **The Tempest**
   Act 3, Scene 3, lines 1-82
   Act 4, Scene 1, lines 56-138

   In the first of these scenes, spirits bring a banquet to Alonso and his followers.
   In the second of these scenes, spirits perform a play for Prospero.

   How does Shakespeare create a magical atmosphere in these two scenes?

   Support your ideas by referring to the extracts.

   (18 marks)

10. **The Tempest**
    Act 2, Scene 1, lines 104-137
    Act 2, Scene 1, lines 197-312

    In the first of these extracts, Sebastian talks to Alonso.
    In the second of these extracts, Sebastian plots with Antonio to kill Alonso.

    What impression of Sebastian's character is given in these scenes?

    Support your ideas by referring to the extracts.

    (18 marks)

Revision Summary Questions

Shakespeare can be really intimidating — especially if you're not used to it. The language is old and funny-looking and often it doesn't seem to make any sense at all. But read this section and have a go, and you'll be able to pick it all up, bit by bit. So make sure you've learned this section well enough to answer all these questions.

1) "You'll get good marks simply by showing you understand what's going on." True or false?
2) How important is it to use lots of quotes?
3) When should you start a new paragraph?
4) Only one of these statements is true. Which one?
   a) You have to understand every single word of Shakespeare to do well in your exam.
   b) You don't have to understand every word — but you do have to know what's happening.
   c) Shakespeare's plays were written in the 1960s by a chartered accountant.
5) What's an Act?
6) What's a Scene?
7) What are the three kinds of plays that Shakespeare wrote?
8) Why do Shakespeare's characters sometimes talk to themselves?
9) What does "[Aside]" mean when you see it in a Shakespeare play?
10) What does "Exeunt" mean?
11) Why is it useful to read the stage directions?
12) What does a director do?
13) Why are Shakespeare's plays written in funny language?
14) What should you do when you see a sentence with the words in a strange order?
15) When you're reading Shakespeare, should you pause at the end of each line, or only when you come to punctuation?
16) If the characters use a lot of words, does that mean they're saying a complicated thing?
17) What does it mean if characters talk in prose?
18) Give one reason why Shakespeare writes in verse.
19) Why might Shakespeare write in rhyming verse?
20) What do "thee" and "thou" mean?
21) What about "thy"? And "hath"?
22) You'll get good marks for showing you understand what Shakespeare's riddles mean. True or false?
23) Why do some of Shakespeare's characters have odd-sounding names?
24) Why do some of the things that happen in Shakespeare's plays seem strange to us?

What You Get in the Exam

These pages will give you a good idea of what to expect in the exam — so you won't get any nasty surprises on the day.

You Have to Write About the *Set Scenes*

You'll study one Shakespeare play for your exam.

You will be told the set scenes for the play you're studying.
The set scenes are important because your exam question will focus on them.

> You have to write about the set scenes in detail in the exam, and show you know them inside-out.

To understand what's going on in the set scenes, you have to know about the rest of the play as well — but not in as much detail.

Here's How the *Shakespeare Question* Works

1) Bits from the scenes will be printed on the exam paper, which is useful — you can remind yourself what happens and get quotes for your essay.
2) Read the scenes through before you try answering the question.
3) Keep looking back to them as you write your answer.
4) This is what the question will look like:

> **The Tempest**
> Act 2, Scene 1, lines 94-137
> Act 3, Scene 3
>
> In these scenes, Alonso faces some disturbing situations.
>
> **What do Alonso's reactions to his problems reveal about his character?**
>
> *Support your ideas by referring to both of the extracts which are printed on the following pages.*

Stick to these bits of the play in your answer. Write about both or you might not get any marks at all.

This means "back up everything you say with quotes". You'll get twice as many marks if you do.

This is the actual question (obviously). Don't write about whatever comes into your head — answer the question.

Be prepared — know the set scenes

Once you've got started, it's not so scary. Read the questions and the bit of the play carefully, use the hints you're given, and above all, don't panic. Then you'll be fine.

Preparing Your Answer

There are two things you've got to do in the exam before you put pen to paper — work out what the question wants, and plan your answer.

Check *Exactly* What the Task is *Asking* For

It's a good idea to start by reading through the bits from the scenes. Now have a good look at exactly what the question is asking you to do.

> **What do we learn about the character of Richard from these scenes?**
> Support your ideas by referring to both of the extracts which are printed on the following pages.

These are the most important words in the question. This is what you have to write about.

1) Go through the scenes again, underlining words that will help answer the question.
2) For this one you'd underline anything that reveals something about Richard's character.
3) Then go through again looking for any less obvious bits about Richard.

Plan Your Essay

Before you start writing, make a plan. This will help you get your points in a sensible order, and it should stop you forgetting anything important.

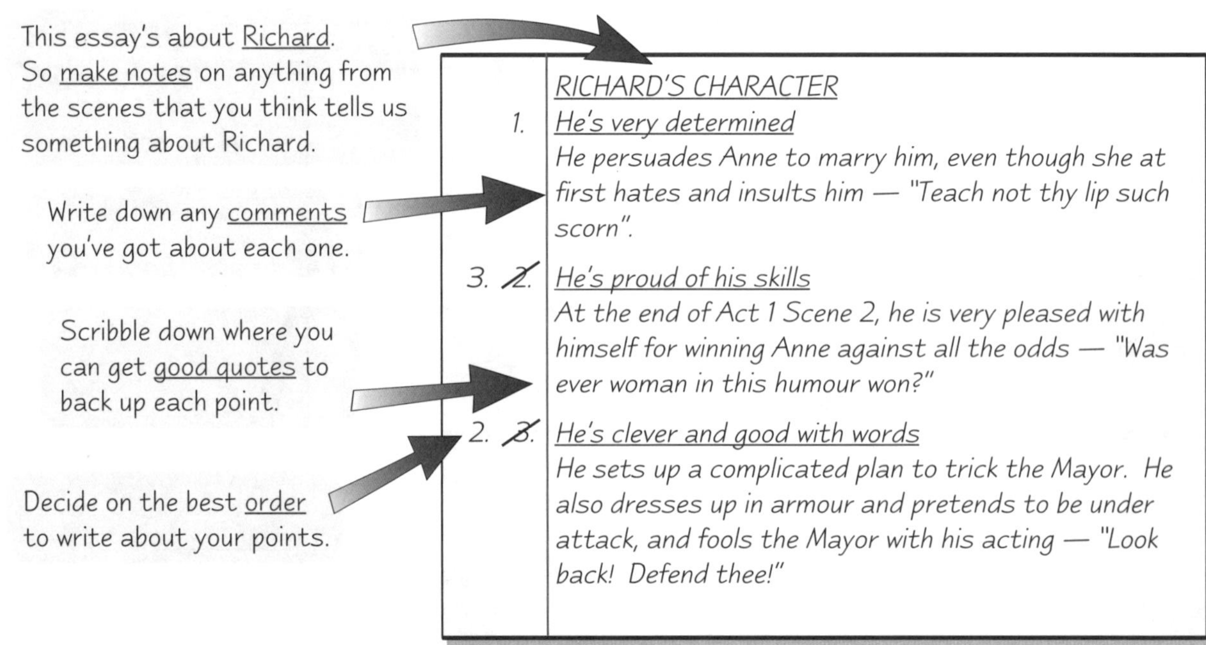

A good answer needs a good plan

You get about 45 minutes for this question — spend at least 10 minutes reading and planning. And remember, if you don't do what the task says, you won't get the marks.

Why Characters Do Things

You can't predict exactly what they'll ask you in the exam — but some types of questions do come up a lot. Questions about the characters and why they do things are pretty common.

Write about ***What They're Like***

Here's an example of the sort of character-based question you might have to answer:

> **Much Ado About Nothing**
> Act 1, Scene 3 and Act 2, Scene 2
>
> **What kind of character is Don John and why does he try to spoil Claudio and Hero's marriage?**
>
> Support your ideas by referring to the scenes.

For this question you need to go through the scenes to find the bits that tell you what Don John is like and what he thinks of Claudio and Hero.

It helps if you go into the exam with a pretty good idea about what the characters are like and what they do in the rest of the play.

Go Through the ***Scenes*** *and* ***Make Notes***

First of all, read through the set scenes again — all the clues you need will be there.

Use evidence from the scenes to back up your points.

Use your knowledge of the play to answer the question.

Don John is pretty nasty. He even calls himself a "plain-dealing villain".

Don John has been beaten in a war by Don Pedro. That's why he hates Claudio — Don Pedro's "right hand" man.

He's in a bad mood in Act 1, Scene 3 and says that ruining Claudio's marriage will make him feel better.

He encourages Borachio to carry out a plan to ruin the marriage — "any impediment will be medicinable to me."

Note down quotes. You'll need them later.

It doesn't have to be a struggle

The exam will feel a lot less like hard work if you keep things simple. The question says exactly what you should do, so do it. The set scenes are right in front of you, so use them. Simple.

Why Characters Do Things

The characters act differently to how you'd expect people to behave in real life. Sometimes this seems odd, but if you know why they're doing it, it really helps you answer the question.

Look for When Characters **Talk About Each Other**

Characters talk about each other — this gives you useful information about them. E.g. Here's what Beatrice and Hero say about Don John in Act 2 Scene 1.

BEATRICE How tartly that gentleman looks! I never can see him but I am heart-burned an hour after.
HERO He is of a very melancholy disposition.

You can find out a lot about the person making the comment as well as the person they're talking about. E.g. Don John sounds pretty bitter when he talks about Claudio.

DON JOHN That young start-up hath all the glory of my overthrow.

Get as Much as You Can from the **Set Scenes**

Remember, you're only expected to write about the bits of the play that they've given you to read. You can find an answer in there, if you look.

If you look at the scenes thoroughly, you can work out a lot about the characters.

Don John doesn't mind being thought of as a bad man. He says in Act 1 Scene 3 that he doesn't see the point of pretending to be nice to people just to make them happy. He even describes himself as a "plain-dealing villain."

Here the character makes it nice and easy for you by describing himself — don't miss these ones.

The characters' actions give you useful clues

Shakespeare uses a few cunning little devices to let you know what the characters are thinking and what they're planning. If you can spot them, it's another thing that'll get you more marks.

Why Characters Do Things

The relationships between the characters are crucial to how Shakespeare's plays work. You have to know how all the characters are connected to each other in the play you're studying.

Remember **Who's Who**

When writing about a character, remember to talk about what their position in society is. It's also important to keep in mind how they're related to the other characters.

> *Don John is illegitimate, so he will never have the wealth and social status which his half-brother Don Pedro has. This is part of the reason why Don John is so bitter and resentful. He is constantly looking for ways to dishonour and humiliate Don Pedro and his friends. He says "to despite them I will endeavour anything."*
>
> *In Shakespeare's time there was a lot of stigma associated with being born outside of marriage. Shakespeare's audience would have expected a character who was illegitimate to be a troublemaker. Don John is therefore a bit of a stereotypical villain.*

Remember to quote to show where your answer comes from.

Write About the **Way** that Characters **Speak**

Shakespeare gives the audience a picture of the characters by what they say and how they say it, just as much as by what they do.

> *Don John talks in prose in these scenes. Shakespeare generally used poetry for the more romantic and distinguished characters and prose for the more ordinary characters. Characters like Claudio and Don Pedro speak a lot in poetry because they're the heroes of the play. The prose spoken by Don John contrasts with this — it emphasises his outsider status from the other nobles.*

Read the scenes carefully to find all the bits that tell you what the characters are like. Pay extra special attention to things they say about each other, and how they speak.

Don't judge the characters by today's standards

You have to judge the characters on the standards of the time. For example, you might think it's wrong that illegitimate children were considered inferior, but social status was a big thing in Shakespeare's time — and this is really important for understanding the plays.

Warm-up and Worked Exam Questions

Before you scurry on to the rest of Section 5, work your way through these pages of questions. The practice'll help you no end in your exam.

Warm-up Questions

1) Give three things that you should do before you even think about writing your answer.
2) If you include quotes in your answer will you get more or fewer marks?
3) Why should you plan your answer?
4) How long should you spend reading and planning?
5) Give three ways in which Shakespeare gives us an idea of what a character is like.

Worked Exam Question

1. **The Tempest**
Act 2, Scene 1, lines 94-137
Act 3, Scene 3
In these scenes, Alonso faces some disturbing situations.

What do Alonso's reactions to his problems reveal about his character?

Support your ideas with references to the extracts.

(18 marks)

Start your essay with a short introduction.

Alonso was involved in the plot to expel Prospero from Milan. He feels very guilty when he realises that his trials on the island are punishment for betraying Prospero. He fears that he has caused his son's death through his actions.

Refer back to the question in your answer

In Act 2, Scene 1, Alonso has been washed up on shore after the storm. He doesn't know what has happened to his son Ferdinand. Alonso reacts to this problem in a very pessimistic way, assuming that his son must have drowned. Francisco tells Alonso that he saw Ferdinand swimming strongly and that he thinks "He came alive to land". However, Alonso refuses to believe Francisco's good news, and says "No, no, he's gone". This reaction shows how gloomy Alonso's character is.

Link your paragraphs together with linking phrases.

In addition to this, in Act 2, Scene 1, Alonso feels sorry for himself because of his problems. For example, he says that he has lost a

Worked Exam Question

Explain what quotes show.

daughter as well as his son because his daughter now lives so far away: "I ne'er again shall see her". This shows a self-pitying side to his character because he is making his problems seem worse they are.

Alonso also reveals a short-tempered aspect to his character in this scene. He interrupts when the other characters are talking, saying "You cram these words into mine ears against / The stomach of my sense". He doesn't want to listen to other people because he is obsessed with his own worries.

Remember to write about both scenes equally.

In Act 3, Scene 3, spirits appear before Alonso and some other characters with a banquet. Alonso says that the banquet might as well be his last meal because he feels the "best is past". This shows how pessimistic he has become because of his problems. Even when something apparently wonderful happens like the banquet, he still feels gloomy.

Start a new paragraph for each new point.

Later in the scene, the banquet disappears and Ariel appears to remind the characters of their crimes against Prospero and to make them feel scared. Ariel claims that Ferdinand is lost and that Alonso will die a slow death on the island. Alonso's reaction to this is very fearful. Gonzalo describes him as standing in a "strange stare". This shows that Alonso lacks bravery. He doesn't look for ways to improve or change his situation, but accepts it passively.

Furthermore, Alonso reacts to Ariel by saying that he wishes he was dead with Ferdinand on the ocean floor and could "with him there lie mudded." This reaction shows how depressed Alonso has become as a result of his experiences on the island.

End your essay with a short conclusion summing up your answer.

In conclusion, Alonso's reactions to his problems on the island reveal a pessimistic character. He always expects the worst and doesn't look for ways to improve his situation.

Exam Questions

Exam Questions

1. **Richard III**
   Act 1, Scene 1, lines 1 to 120
   Act 3, Scene 7, lines 111 to 173

   In these extracts, we see two sides to Richard's personality — his dishonesty and also his cleverness.

   Explain how much you think we can admire Richard in these extracts.

   Support your ideas with references to the extracts.

   (18 marks)

2. **Much Ado About Nothing**
   Act 1, Scene 1, lines 85 to 129
   Act 4, Scene 1, line 253 to end of scene
   Act 5, Scene 4, lines 67 to 97

   How does the relationship between Benedick and Beatrice change during the course of the play?

   In your answer you should comment on:
   - how the characters' feelings towards each other change
   - the language the characters use when they speak to each other

   Support your ideas by referring to the extracts.

   (18 marks)

3. **The Tempest**
   Act 1, Scene 2, line 447 to end of scene
   Act 3, Scene 1, line 48 to end of scene

   In these scenes, Miranda meets Ferdinand and falls in love with him.

   What impression of Miranda's character is given in these scenes?

   Support your ideas by referring to the extracts.

   (18 marks)

Imagine You're Directing a Scene

The director is the boss of the play — he or she is in charge of all the important stuff to do with how the play looks, sounds and feels.

*Think about the **Audience***

Directing a play means deciding how you want to show the story to the audience.

The actors have to play their parts so that the audience understand what's happening. The director tells the actors how they have to do this. The director also makes decisions about lots of other things which affect how the play comes across.

*The Audience **Don't** Have the **Script** in Front of Them*

You have to make the audience understand what's happening, and your answer should say how you'd do this. Here are some ideas:

1) Make the actors say their lines in a way that shows the feelings of the character.

Angry shouting

2) Show the audience what a character is like by the clothes or make-up they wear.

Evil clothes

3) Show the audience the mood of a scene by your choice of set, lighting and sound.

Romantic setting

Questions about directing let you be creative

Shakespeare was often quite vague about things like tone of voice, lighting and sound — so there's plenty of scope for being imaginative. The costumes you choose can be modern clothing if you like — as long as you can explain why that costume is suitable.

Imagine You're Directing a Scene

Questions about being the director can be quite fun, because you can be really creative. Before you start to answer one though, you need to have a good understanding of the scene.

*You Have to **Understand** the **Scene***

Once again, you have to understand what's going on, because you have to say how you would show the audience what's going on.

That means you need to understand the language.

ARIEL The pow'rs, delaying, not forgetting, have
Incensed the seas and shores, yea, all the creatures,
Against your peace.

Ariel is telling Alonso and his followers that they're going to be punished in lots of weird and nasty ways for betraying Prospero — pretty scary stuff.

If you don't understand what a character's talking about, it's very difficult to tell if they're sad, happy or angry.

*Back Up Your Points with **Quotes***

These questions are a bit different from other types of exam questions, but one thing is the same — you absolutely have to quote. This makes your ideas much stronger.

If you want an actor to speak a line in a particular way, then write that down. Give a quote.

When Caliban describes to Stephano how to kill Prospero, he could speak the line, "There thou mayst brain him", in a secretive whisper. This would show he knows what he's saying could get him into trouble.

Quote a bit of the scene that really shows you what the mood of that scene is.

Explain why your directions are a good idea

Just because these questions are more open to interpretation than other questions, that doesn't mean you can say whatever you want. Your ideas have to be sensible, and you should always explain why you think your ideas are suitable for the scene.

Imagine You're Directing a Scene

The audience should feel all the different moods that Shakespeare wanted them to feel when he wrote the play. In your answer, you have to write about how you'd create these moods.

*Write About the **Mood** of the Scene*

The mood of the scene is really important for this type of question. Some scenes are funny, some are scary, some are full of excitement and tension, and some are romantic.

The mood of this scene is bleak and gloomy — Alonso is convinced his son has drowned, and says he just wants to find him and die with him. He should speak in a grim, serious tone to emphasise this mood.

O, it is monstrous, monstrous!
Methought the billows spoke, and told me of it,
The winds did sing it to me and the thunder,
That deep and dreadful organ-pipe, pronounced
The name of Prosper — it did bass my trespass.
Therefore my son i' th' ooze is bedded, and
I'll seek him deeper than e'er plummet sounded,
And with him there lie mudded.

*Find the **Moodiest Parts** of the Scene*

The mood of the scene you get will be pretty clear. What you have to do in your answer is say which bits show the mood of the scene more than others.

The main speeches are often a good place to start for this. But you also get clues about the mood from other places, such as stage directions.

For the bits of the scene that you've picked out, first explain why you think they're important to the mood.

Then say how you would bring this mood out. Say what tone of voice the characters should speak in, what kind of lighting you'd use, talk about the set — anything that would help create an atmosphere.

Think about what the audience will see

The trick to writing about directing a scene is to think about the audience's point of view. You have to show them what the mood of the scene is — this is the director's job.

How Characters Persuade

You might get a question about how characters persuade — especially for a play like *Richard III* where there are lots of big speeches. The next two pages look at this kind of question.

Here's a Classic **Persuading Question**

Richard III
Act 1, Scene 2, lines 114-224
Act 5, Scene 3, line 303 to end of scene

How does Richard use persuasive language to woo Anne and motivate his troops in these extracts?

Support your ideas with references to the following extracts.

1) To make your answer really good you'll have to make several points in your answer.
2) The main things you can write about for this question are the language Richard uses and the effect it has on all the other characters who appear in these two scenes.

1) Write about the **Tricks** of **Persuasive Language**

This is where you get to write about all the tricks of Shakespeare's language. Look through the extracts you're given in the question and find some quotes which show persuasive language:

RICHARD Your beauty was the cause of that effect —
Your beauty, that did haunt me in my sleep
To undertake the death of all the world,
So I might live one hour in your sweet bosom.

Richard plays down his crimes and flatters Anne by using romantic language. He claims he only acted badly because he was so in love with Anne.

ANNE I would I knew thy heart.
RICHARD 'Tis figured in my tongue.
ANNE I fear me both are false.
RICHARD Then never was man true.

He shows he's keen by persistently responding to Anne's criticism.

RICHARD Remember whom you are to cope withal —
A sort of vagabonds, rascals and runaways,
A scum of Britains and base lackey peasants

Richard motivates his army by insulting their enemies, saying they're uncivilised and immoral.

RICHARD Shall these enjoy our lands?
Lie with our wives?
Ravish our daughters?

He makes his troops afraid of what might happen if they lose the battle.

RICHARD Advance our standards, set upon our foes.
Our ancient word of courage, fair Saint George,
Inspire us with the spleen of fiery dragons!
Upon them! Victory sits on our helms.

He finishes his speech with patriotic, optimistic language to get his army in the mood for fighting.

How Characters Persuade

Write about What He's Trying to **Do**

When you plan your answer, make sure you understand what the character's purpose is.
Make sure you know who they're trying to persuade and what they want to persuade them of.
Try to show you know how the extracts fit in with the rest of the play.

> *In Act 1 Scene 2, Richard's powers of persuasion are put to the test when he asks Anne to marry him, despite admitting to killing her husband Prince Edward. At first she seems disgusted by him and responds angrily to his attempts to woo her...*

Say **How** He Tries to **Persuade** People

Next you need to say what techniques the character uses to try and get what they want.
Use the quotes you've found and explain what they show you about the methods of persuasion.

> *Richard tries to flatter Anne by using lots of romantic language to say how beautiful she is. He tells her that her eyes "have drawn salt tears" from him, deliberately presenting himself as a sensitive, caring man. He pleads with Anne, "Teach not thy lip such scorn", suggesting that he is hurt by the way she has treated him.*

Remember to explain the effect of the quotes you use.

Say **How Successful** He is

It's a good idea to comment on how effective the character's skills of persuasion are.
One way to judge this is to look at how other characters respond.

> *Despite Anne's initial hostility, Richard's persuasive skills are so strong that he eventually wins her over. Richard's words are so effective that Anne is convinced that he has "become so penitent". She is totally taken in by Richard, believing so strongly that he is a changed man that she eventually agrees to marry him.*

Say why you think the character's attempts to persuade are effective or not..

Look at the effect of the characters' words

There are two things you have to write about for persuasion questions — the words the character uses, and what the other characters say and do in reaction to their words.

Warm-up and Worked Exam Questions

Persuasion and direction questions can be on the difficult side. Get your eye in with these warm-up questions before you have a look at how to answer a real question.

Warm-up Questions

1) What sort of things would you write about if a question asked you to imagine you were directing a scene?
2) True or False?
   If you write about directing a scene you don't have to understand the language.
3) If you are writing about the mood of a scene, what should you write about?
   a) How stroppy the actors are
   b) How the scene makes the audience feel
   c) How many characters are in it
4) Name one of the language tricks you might easily spot in a piece of persuasive language.

Writing about how characters persuade each other is a popular topic for a Shakespeare question. The example question below is based on a scene from *Much Ado About Nothing*.

Worked Exam Question

Much Ado About Nothing
Act 4, Scene 1, line 110 to end of scene

In this scene, characters are using their powers of persuasion.
Friar Francis is trying to persuade Leonato that things are not as bad as they seem, and Beatrice is trying to persuade Benedick to challenge Claudio.

Write about the ways the Friar and Beatrice set out to persuade, commenting on how successful they are.

Support your ideas by referring to the extract.

(18 marks)

The question is split into two parts — one about the Friar and the other about Beatrice. So plan your answer in two parts.

Notes

Friar v.calm — confident Hero's innocent — says he's been watching her — lists signs of innocence — reminds L. he's an experienced priest — explains his plan which works 2 ways — v. reassuring — describes H.'s goodness — succeeds

Beatrice much more passionate — wants revenge — tempts B. — asks him to prove his love, threatens to leave — rages about Claudio (calls him names) — says she'd kill him if she was a man — Ben. can't get a word in — says she's positive Hero is innocent — succeeds.

Worked Exam Question

Worked Exam Question

The methods of persuasion used by Friar Francis and Beatrice reflect their differing personalities.

Just a brief intro is enough.

Leonato is furious when Claudio rejects Hero. He believes that Hero is guilty straight away and says "Death is the fairest cover for her shame". This shows what a state he is in, but Friar Francis stays calm and comforts Hero. He shows he is confident of her innocence. When Leonato criticises Hero for even looking up, the Friar says "Yea, wherefore should she not?" The fact that he doesn't seem to doubt Hero is reassuring.

As always, use plenty of quotes, and explain each one.

He lets Leonato rant on about Hero, talking about her "foul tainted flesh," and when Leonato seems to have finished, the Friar explains that he has been silent because he has been watching Hero closely. He says he has been "noting of the lady." He then begins to list the little signs of innocence he has noted in Hero's manner, such as her blushing. It is very methodical and convincing. He also reminds him that he's an experienced priest. This helps Leonato to trust what he says:

"trust not my age,
My reverence, calling, nor divinity,
If this sweet lady lie not guiltless here"
(Act 4, Scene 1, 165-167)

When you quote more than one line, put the quote in a separate paragraph and say where the quote is from.

The Friar convinces Leonato by saying his plan would work even if Hero was guilty. He also reminds Leonato of Hero's sweet nature by describing how upset Claudio will be when he thinks Hero's dead. In the end Leonato agrees to the plan, although he does say it's because he's so upset he can't really argue: "The smallest twine may lead me."

Join the two halves of your answer with a good linking sentence.

So the Friar persuades Leonato through calm and logic; Beatrice, on the other hand, is much more emotional. She wants Benedick to kill Claudio in revenge. Because he loves her, he is tempted by her statement, "Ah, how much might a man deserve of me that would right her!". When he has declared he loves her, she asks him to kill Claudio as proof and threatens to leave when he hesitates, saying "In faith, I will go."

When Benedick asks if Claudio is really her enemy she begins raging about him and exclaiming "Oh God that I were a man!" She shows the violence of her feelings by saying "I would eat his heart in the market place" which convinces Benedick that she's serious. When Benedick finally gets a chance to ask if she really believes Hero is innocent, she answers very simply, "Yea, as sure as I have a thought, or a soul." She sounds very sincere. He finally agrees and says "I will challenge him".

Both the Friar and Beatrice were equally successful in their persuasion, but the Friar used reason and logic while Beatrice's methods of persuasion were driven by passion and emotion.

In the final paragraph, sum up your main points, and make sure you answer the question.

Exam Questions

Exam Questions

1. **The Tempest**
   Act 1, Scene 2, lines 411-468
   Act 5, Scene 1, lines 33-103

   Imagine you are going to direct these scenes in a school production of *The Tempest.*

   What instructions would you give the actor playing Prospero about how he should speak and move during these two scenes?

   Support your ideas by referring to the extracts.

   (18 marks)

2. **Richard III**
   Act 1, Scene 1, lines 1 to 43
   Act 3, Scene 7, lines 141 to 247

   Imagine you are going to direct these extracts for a class performance.

   What instructions would you give to the actor playing Richard in these extracts, in order to show his dishonesty?

   Support your ideas by referring to the extracts.

   (18 marks)

3. **Much Ado About Nothing**
   Act 4, Scene 1, lines 1 to 105
   Act 5, Scene 4, lines 1 to 71

   Imagine that you are directing a performance of these two extracts.

   Explain what decisions you would make about how the characters should speak and move.

   Support your ideas by referring to the extracts.

   (18 marks)

Writing about a Theme

Theme questions sound harder than they really are. They're just asking how the play puts across a particular message or idea.

Work Out What the Question is *Asking*

Theme questions are often worded like this:

> **Much Ado About Nothing**
>
> **Act 4, Scene 1, lines 108-198 and Act 5, Scene 1, lines 45-105**
> In these scenes, Leonato and Antonio are devastated by the accusations about Hero.
> **How do these extracts show the importance of honour and reputation?**
> *Support your ideas by referring to the extracts.*

You could rephrase this as: "These bits of the play show that honour and reputation are important. How do they do this?"

Don't panic if the question seems complicated.
Read it carefully, and you'll realise it's actually pretty simple.

Theme Questions Aren't as Hard as they Look

1) Read through the scenes with the question in mind, and some points should pretty much leap out at you and give you the basis for a good answer.
For example, for the question above, this quote from Leonato would be useful:

> Wherefore? Why, doth not every earthly thing
> Cry shame upon her? Could she here deny
> The story that is printed in her blood?
> Do not live, Hero, do not ope thine eyes;
> For did I think thou wouldst not quickly die,
> Thought I thy spirits were stronger than thy shames,
> Myself would on the rearward of reproaches
> Strike at thy life.

2) Once you've found a good extract like this, just say how it relates to the question. Don't forget to stick in some good quotes to back up your points:

> *Leonato is so concerned about losing his good reputation that he would rather Hero died than for the stories about her to become known. He harshly tells her "do not ope thine eyes", without even giving her the chance to deny the accusations.*

Writing about a Theme

Here are a few more things you can do if you get a question about a theme or an issue.

Each Play has **Several Main Themes**

If you get a theme question, depending on the play, it's likely to be about one of these:

RICHARD III

- good and evil
- royalty
- dreams and prophecy
- crimes and guilt
- loyalty
- history

MUCH ADO ABOUT NOTHING

- honour and reputation
- tricks and disguises
- love and marriage
- evil
- innocence
- wit

THE TEMPEST

- fate and justice
- magic
- love
- freedom
- betrayal and forgiveness
- slavery and service

Look for the **Less Obvious** Bits

1) There are usually plenty of fairly obvious points you can use in your answer to a theme question.
2) If you want really good marks you'll need to go into a bit more detail. Try to write something that answers the question in a way that's not immediately obvious.

> *Maybe Prospero himself was only getting what he deserved when he lost his position as Duke of Milan. He admits that he was so obsessed with learning that he became guilty of "neglecting worldly ends". This seems to be what allowed Antonio's "falsehood" to develop — if Prospero had paid more attention to his duties, it is possible that Antonio would not have had the chance to abuse his trust.*

3) It's especially important to give evidence for these kinds of points. The examiner might not be sure what you're referring to, so it's vital that you back it up with good quotations.
4) Don't go over the top trying to write really original stuff — make sure you don't miss the clear-cut points that'll give you easy marks. But if you can stick just one or two more unexpected, well-explained points into your plan, along with the easier stuff, they'll make your answer really stand out.

Well it all themes thimple enough...

There's usually loads you can say about the main themes of each of the set texts. But remember — if you don't give any evidence then you're not going to get good marks for it. And don't forget, there's no wrong answer, as long as you've got a quote to back it up.

Writing Your Answer

All the questions are different, but there are a few basic points that'll help you do any of them.

Watch Your **Paragraphs**, **Sentences** and **Spelling**

It's no good understanding the play if you don't write well.
Here are some tips on impressing the examiner with what you write.

1) Think about what you want to say, and make sure your sentences are good and clear.
2) Every time you make a new point, start a new paragraph.
3) Link your points together well and link them to the question.
4) Take care with those spellings.

Use phrases like "Another way that Shakespeare creates tension is..."

Don't Forget to **Quote**

Quoting is the key. If you don't quote, you won't get the marks — it really is that simple.
Remember, the whole purpose of quoting is to back up a point you've made.

Here's an example:

> *Queen Margaret clearly hates Richard. While watching him arguing with Elizabeth, Margaret makes several comments about him, unheard by the other characters, which suggest a bitter argument is to come:*
> *"Hie thee to hell for shame, and leave this world,*
> *Thou cacodemon! there thy kingdom is."*
> *Act 1, Scene 3, 142-143*

If you're quoting more than one line, put the quote in a separate paragraph.

Follow this rule and you'll write a good answer:

Make a point, give a quote and explain why you've used the quote.

Quoting well makes all the difference

In every single paragraph, aim to quote. You'd have to be pretty daft if you forgot to quote after reading this page. If you quote well in your SAT, you're onto a winner.

Warm-up and Worked Exam Questions

Warm-up time, methinks.

Warm-up Questions

1) Which of these sentences give good advice for writing about themes?
   a) You can spot theme questions because they always have the word 'theme' in them.
   b) Always put in quotes to back up your points.
   c) There are some obvious main themes for each of the set plays.
   d) Only go for the really obvious things — don't bother with less-obvious bits.
2) Which of these sentences give good advice about quoting?
   a) You don't have to quote unless you can be bothered.
   b) If you're quoting more than one line, put the quote in a separate paragraph.
   c) You should use quotes to back up your points.

Here's an extract from an answer where you have to write about the theme of love.

Worked Exam Question

1. **Much Ado About Nothing**
   Act 1 Scene 1, lines 190 to 247
   Act 2 Scene 3, lines 137 to 200

   In these extracts, Claudio and Don Pedro talk about Benedick's attitude to women and love.

   How does the language in these extracts create a humorous attitude to love?

   In the first extract Shakespeare creates a humorous attitude to love using word play, for example when Benedick says "how short his answer is — with Hero, Leonato's short daughter". He also uses exaggeration to make Benedick's declarations that he'll never fall in love funnier; "If I do, hang me in a bottle like a cat and shoot at me". This sort of language gives the impression of three young men teasing each other about love in a very light-hearted way. In the second extract Shakespeare also uses exaggeration to create comedy on the theme of love; "beats her heart, tears her hair, prays, curses, "O sweet Benedick!" This seems so ridiculous to the audience, knowing Beatrice's character, that it is particularly funny when Benedick believes that Beatrice has said it.

Exam Questions

Exam Questions

1. **Much Ado About Nothing**
   Act 3, Scene 4
   Act 4, Scene 1, lines 1 to 204

   In the first of these extracts, we see Hero preparing for her wedding. In the second extract, Claudio rejects her at the altar.

   How do these extracts show the importance of honour and reputation in the play?

   Support your ideas by referring to the extracts.

   (18 marks)

2. **Much Ado About Nothing**
   Act 2, Scene 2
   Act 4, Scene 1, lines 204-258

   Both these scenes contain plots to deceive Claudio and Don Pedro, but for very different purposes.

   How do these two extracts show how tricks can be used for both good and evil purposes?

   Support your ideas by referring to the extracts.

   (18 marks)

3. **The Tempest**
   Act 1, Scene 2, lines 294-376
   Act 5, Scene 1, lines 83-103

   In the first scene, Caliban complains bitterly about having to serve Prospero. In the second scene, Ariel is happy that he might soon have his freedom.

   How is the theme of slavery explored in these scenes?

   Support your ideas by referring to the extracts.

   (18 marks)

Exam Questions

Exam Questions

4. **The Tempest**
   Act 3, Scene 3, line 52 to end of scene
   Act 5, Scene 1, lines 58-181

   In the first of these scenes, Antonio, Alonso and Sebastian are confronted about their crime against Prospero. In the second of these scenes, Prospero decides to forgive them.

   How does Shakespeare explore ideas about guilt and forgiveness in these scenes?

   Support your ideas by referring to the extracts.

   (18 marks)

5. **Richard III**
   Act 1, Scene 1, lines 42 to 121
   Act 3, Scene 7, lines 95 to 173

   In these extracts, Richard uses deception to gain the trust of other characters.

   How do these scenes show that appearances can be deceptive?

   Support your ideas with reference to the extracts.

   (18 marks)

6. **Richard III**
   Act 1, Scene 3, lines 215-322
   Act 5, Scene 1

   In Act 1, Scene 3, Queen Margaret curses everyone. In Act 5, Scene 1, Buckingham remembers the curse.

   How do the curses and omens mentioned in these scenes explore the theme of prophecy in the play?

   Support your ideas by referring to the extracts.

   (18 marks)

Revision Summary Questions

If you've learnt all the advice in this section, you should feel a lot more confident that you can give a good answer for the Shakespeare Question. Go through all the questions on this page to check you know everything. As always, if you get stuck, go back through the section to find the answers you're not sure of — then do the questions again until you can do them all.

1) Which of these statements is true?
   a) You only need to know the set scenes and nothing else.
   b) You need to know the whole play in detail.
   c) You need to know the set scenes really well, and the rest of the play in less detail.
2) Why is it important to make a plan for your answer?
3) Why is it a good idea to read through the set scenes again before starting your answer?
4) Why is it really useful to find a bit of the play where the characters talk about each other?
5) Name two more things you should write about when you're describing why characters do things.
6) What does the director do?
   a) The director writes the play.
   b) The director decides how to show the play to the audience.
   c) The director makes tea and scones for the actors.
7) As a director:
   a) What could you change to show the emotions a character is feeling?
   b) How could you show what a character is like?
   c) How could you alter the mood of a scene?
8) True or false:
   "You don't have to quote when answering a question about directing a scene."
9) Where might you look to find clues about the mood of the scene?
   a) The speeches and the stage directions.
   b) In the margins.
   c) Right at the end of the scene.
10) Which of these is spelled correctly?
   a) Persausive langauge.
   b) Persuasive language.
   c) Parsuasive language.
11) What should you do after each point you make in your answer?
12) What are the two main things you should look at in persuasion questions?
13) What are two of the important themes in your set play?
14) True or false:
   "You can get great marks just by pointing out the obvious bits for a theme question."
15) True or false:
   "Quotes should always be in a separate paragraph."

What You Have to Do

Writing Questions can be quite tricky. Here are some ways to make them easier.

You Have to Do **Two Writing Questions**

There are two parts to the Writing Paper:

1) The Long Writing Question: you have to read a short bit of writing which sets the scene, then write something connected with that bit of writing.

2) The Short Writing Question: there's a short bit of writing which sets the scene, then a task that's based on it.

IN THE EXAM: Don't rush into doing the writing. Read the questions carefully before you start.

Show Off These **Five** Things in Your Writing

The examiners want to see how good you are at the nuts and bolts of writing. Here's what they're looking for:

1) **Good Spelling**
So always check over what you've written for mistakes.

2) **Proper sentences**
Use correct punctuation in all your sentences, so that they make sense.

3) **Well-organised writing**
That means writing in paragraphs, having an introduction and a clear ending, and a sensible order to all the points you make in between.

4) **The right style**
E.g. If you're asked for a magazine article use words and phrases that make your writing sound like a magazine article.

5) **Signs you've thought about the reader**
If it's a piece for young kids keep it simple so they can understand. If it's for your gran don't put in any swearing. Make sure it's interesting enough to keep your reader from nodding off too.

Keep it simple and you'll be fine

Writing Questions don't have to be really hard. Take a deep breath, read through the questions carefully, and remember what they're looking for — good writing, not amazing ideas.

The Long Writing Question

The two Writing Questions aren't wildly different. But they're not exactly the same either — learn the difference now so you don't make any unfortunate boobs on the day.

The **Long Writing** Question Looks Like This

There's quite a lot to read for these tasks. Read through it all carefully a couple of times, so you know exactly what they want you to do.

> This is an extract from the newspaper the *Daily Hail*.
>
> ***The Daily Hail***
>
> **Fur Will Fly at No.10**
>
> *The Editor writes:*
> What's going on at 10 Downing Street? First we learn that Humphrey the cat's not allowed in the offices. Now we learn he's been confined to the kitchen. And there's no cat flap. What kind of life is this for a cat that's served the nation for nine and a half years? I'm disgusted, Prime Minister, and I believe the British public is disgusted too.
>
> **As a reader of the *Daily Hail*, write a letter to the Prime Minister, agreeing or disagreeing with the article.**

This bit of writing sets the scene. Read it carefully.

This is what you've actually got to do.

So, to answer this question you've got to:

1) Pretend you're someone who reads the "Daily Hail".
2) Write a letter to the Prime Minister.
   Use the right language, and lay it out like a proper letter.
3) EITHER agree with the article OR disagree with the article.

What You **Need** to **Know**

You should spend about 45 minutes on this question.
Spend about 15 minutes planning. Spend about 25 minutes writing.
Leave about 5 minutes at the end to check over what you've written.

It's called the long Writing Question, but you don't have to write pages and pages. A bit over 300 words should do it.

You'll be able to use ideas from the article to work out what you're going to say.

For this question, you could pick out all the points the editor makes, then agree or disagree with each point.

The Short Writing Question

This page tells you exactly what to expect from the Short Writing Question, and how to answer it.

The Short Writing Question Looks Like This

It starts with a short introduction to the topic.

Then there's a bit setting the scene for the piece you've got to write.

You'll get a few hints about what to write about. These hints are really helpful — use them.

If they say article they mean article. Don't go writing a letter or a speech.

> Some teachers at your school are worried that pupils are under too much pressure to achieve high grades.
>
> ---
>
> *The following is printed in your school newspaper:*
>
> We want to know what you think about pressure at school.
>
> Tell us whether you find school stressful or not. Do you feel under pressure from teachers, in exams or on the sports field?
>
> Do your parents put you under pressure to do well? If so, what effect is all this stress having on you?
>
> **Write the article for the school newspaper.**

What You Need to Know

1) You get 20 marks for this task.
2) Spend about 10 minutes planning and 20 minutes writing.
3) You need to write about 200 words for this one. Keep your writing organised and stick to the point. You haven't got time to write a long waffly essay.

Use the Hints You're Given

- Time's short.
- They give marks for how well you write, not for brilliant ideas.
- Using the hints in the question is the quickest way to get started.

Do exactly what the question asks you to do

The two Writing Questions are a bit different, so you have to tackle them in different ways. Make sure you follow the instructions word for word.

Work Out What to Say

Once you've read the question, work out what you're going to say to answer it.
That means making a plan.

Decide What to Say **Before** You Start

You've got to have a good think about what you're going to write about before you start.
You don't need to know exactly what you're going to write, but you need to have a rough idea.

Good writing makes a point. It doesn't just ramble on about nothing.

Whether you're writing a story, a description, a letter or an opinion piece, make sure you've got enough ideas to keep you writing till your time's up — without having to waffle.

Jot Down Your Points into a **Rough Plan**

It's a good idea to jot down a plan of the points you want to make before you start writing.
That way you don't get to the end and realise you've forgotten something.

Q. Write an article for a newspaper about an issue that's important to you.
Explain why you think the issue is important.

PLAN: Modern farming methods.

Reducing quality of soil — less food can be grown — soon we won't have enough to eat.

Risks to human health — pesticides — antibiotics in meat.

Animals treated badly — profits more important than welfare.

What we can do — buy organic.

A plan doesn't have to be in proper sentences. It's just a reminder for you to use.

Start with what you think is the most important point. This grabs your reader's attention.

Try to link your points together. You can link smoothly from meat to treatment of animals.

Work out how you're going to end your piece.
This is a positive ending — it says what we can do.

Keep your answer to the point

Obviously, writing that rambles on without getting anywhere isn't going to get the best marks.
Work out roughly what you're going to say before you start writing. It helps to jot down a plan.
All this needs to be second nature by the time you get to the exam, so get learning.

Warm-up Questions

Have a go at these warm-up questions. They should help you check you've taken in all the stuff in this section so far.

Warm-up Questions

1) How many Writing Questions do you have to do in your exam?

2) What is the main difference between them, besides how much time you get for each one?

3) Imagine you have been asked to write an information leaflet for elderly people, which gives them advice about keeping warm in winter.
Which of these beginnings would be most suitable?

   a) *Yo dudes! For all you grannies and grandpas out there, here's the plan for keeping roasty toasty this winter!*

   b) *High heating bills can make winter a worrying time for all of us, but there's no need to be anxious. This leaflet will tell you how to keep warm without breaking the bank.*

4) How much are you expected to write in the longer writing task?

   a) A paragraph should do the trick — but it has to be a perfect one.

   b) Aim for about 300 words. Keep to the point and choose your words carefully.

   c) Write loads. If you have to ask for extra paper you know you're on for a level 7.

5) Which of the following are forms they might ask you to write in for your exam?

article	**triangle**	**letter**
speech	**story**	**driving licence application**

6) Which is more important in the writing task — earth-shatteringly brilliant original ideas, or a well organised and interesting writing style?

7) What should you do if a question gives you a list of things you should write about?

8) a) You will get 15 minutes planning time in the longer writing task.
   What should you use it for?

   b) Do you need to plan for the shorter writing task?

9) What should you use the last five minutes of the Writing exam for?

Stories Need Planning Too

It's not just the questions which ask for your opinion that need planning. You should also make a plan if you're doing a story question. Even description pieces will be better with a plan.

Plan What Will Happen In Your Story

It's tempting just to start by writing "once upon a time..." and hope that you'll be able to make up what happens in your story as you go along. But that's a really bad idea.

Before you start to write your story, you should have a good idea of how it's going to end, and what's going to happen in the middle. Otherwise you'll get in all sorts of problems.

Q. Write about an exciting journey you have made.
It can be real or imaginary.

PLAN: Going on holiday on a plane.

Everyone except me got very ill from the food.

Went to the cockpit — pilot was unconscious.

I talked to air traffic control over the pilot's radio and they told me what to do.

I landed the plane safely.

Everyone went to hospital — they were all fine.

This plan is like a summary of the story you're going to write.

When you write the story, you could have two or three paragraphs about each of these points.

You've planned how it's going to end, so you always know what you're aiming towards.

Even Description Pieces Need a Plan

When you're describing something, there isn't a beginning, a middle and an end like in a story. But you still need to know what kind of things you're going to say.

Q. Describe your favourite place.

PLAN: Down by the river — peaceful and pretty — lots of grass — friends — go swimming in summer — ice skating in winter — friendly horse in nearby field — lots of trees — lovely colours in autumn — wild flowers in spring.

It might not look like much, but notes like this can really help you.
You're not going to get stuck and panic because you've run out of ideas for things to write.

A plan is like a safety net

Whatever it is you've got to write, having a plan can really help you. If you start writing without a plan, you're likely to run out of ideas or find you're waffling on about nothing at all.

Use the Right Style

Using the right writing style to write your answer is very important. You'll lose marks if you choose the wrong style, or if you change styles halfway through your answer.

Write in a **Style** that **Fits** the Question

Each question needs you to write in a certain style. Look at what the question is telling you to do, and use your common sense to decide what style to write in.

Golden sandy beaches and gently lapping waves await you on the island of Noonos. Soak up the sun and forget your worldly cares with a refreshing swim in the warm, crystal-clear sea...

If you're asked to write a travel brochure, use loads of fancy phrases — like this.

The faulty pelican crossing has caused ten accidents. Do you want to run that risk? We must take action now before someone else is injured — or even killed. Write to your local councillor at once.

If the question tells you to write a speech, be snappy, punchy and direct — like this.

Slowly, the thick oak door creaked open. Emma quaked with fear. The clock ticked loudly. Then — bang! The ear-piercing crack of a gunshot filled the room. Emma screamed.

If the question tells you to write a horror story, use words that give a feeling of fear and suspense — like this.

Use **Fancy Words** if You **Need** Them

Some writing styles tend to involve lots of fancy words.
Don't be afraid to use them — but only if you're sure you know what they mean.

The important thing is to show you know what kind of style you're supposed to be using.
You'll get marks for trying — even if the spelling of the longer words is a bit wonky.

Choosing the right style shows you understand

It's vital that you get the style right — or at least that you show you understand what sort of style you should be using. Make sure that's in your mind when you answer the question.

Writing Letters

It's especially important to get your writing style right when you have to write a letter.
If you're asked to write a letter, sort out whether it's formal or informal.

Formal Letters need Formal Language

Formal letters are to people you don't know very well.
They are things like a letter of complaint, a letter requesting information, or a letter from a head teacher to a parent.

Q. Write a letter to a supermarket manager complaining about poor quality food you bought at their store.

Dear Sir/Madam,

I wish to inform you that I contracted food poisoning from a fish finger bought at your store. I purchased the item on Saturday March 14th and consumed it that night. It made me severely ill for several days.

Yours faithfully,

Osborn Outhouse (Mr.)

The letter uses long words and the tone is very formal.

Obviously you'd write much more than this in the exam.

Be specific about places and times.

If you start a formal letter "Dear Sir/Madam," always end with "Yours faithfully". If you know the name of the person you're writing to, use "Yours sincerely".

Use Formal Expressions

This is the sort of phrase you might use in a formal letter:

- In my opinion
- I find this state of affairs appalling/outrageous/unsatisfactory
- I was surprised to discover...
- May I take this opportunity to congratulate you on...

Don't throw marks away by using the wrong style

It sounds obvious, but it's easy to forget: when you write a formal letter, use a formal style.
Try to get all the conventions right, like the way you start and end the letter.

Writing Letters

If you're asked to write an informal letter — e.g. to a friend — you should use an informal style of writing. This will make it feel more realistic, and get you more marks.

Informal Letters are *Chatty*

Letters to your friends are informal. You know your friends well — so you don't need to use formal language with them. Write in a chatty style, like you'd use if you were talking to them.

Q. Write a letter to a friend about something that happened to you recently.

Dear Fred,

I've been feeling rotten these last few days. I ate a dodgy fish finger from the store. It whistled right through my system, I can tell you. I was throwing up all night. I'd steer well clear of them if I were you, mate.

See you soon,

Ossie

There's no need to give your full name — your friends know who you are.

The language is very chatty and informal. You wouldn't write this way to a stranger.

Don't end informal letters with "Yours faithfully" or "Yours sincerely". Write something like "love" or "best wishes" instead.

Use *Everyday* Expressions

You'll probably find it comes more naturally to you to write in an informal style. Think about how you talk to your friends in real life — just because it's an exam, it doesn't mean you can't use everyday speech when it's appropriate.

Get a feel for the letter

If the question asks you to write a letter, stop and think about who the letter is to. If your letter is to someone you don't know, use formal language — if it's to a friend, use a more chatty style.

Warm-up Questions

These warm-up questions will help you remember some good advice for the Writing Paper. You don't know what they're going to ask you, but the basic rules for this paper will stay the same.

Warm-up Questions

1) Is this statement true or false?
   You don't need to plan a story — that's what makes it interesting.

2) Do descriptions need to be planned?

3) Would you say the following is good advice?
   Take a risk by including interesting words you know, even if you're not 100% sure of the spellings.

4) Your writing style needs to fit the task.
   Read the three beginnings a) to c), then match them to the correct purpose i) to iii):

   i) to **entertain** ii) to **persuade** iii) to **inform**

   a) Are you horrified by your gas bill? Are you always turning the heating down? Do you wish you had more money to spend on things you really wanted?

   b) Dear Sir or Madam,
   I am writing to let you know that there will be an increase in the cost of domestic gas as from the end of September.

   c) The gas bill slithered through the letter box as silently as a snake and lay in wait for me on the mat.

5) What does writing style involve? (There is more than one correct answer.)

   a) different types of sentences (questions, statements, etc.)
   b) a good quality pen
   c) sentence length
   d) your choice of words and phrases

6) Imagine you have been asked to write a letter to each of these people.
   Put them into two groups:

   Group 1 — you would write **formally** to these people.

   Group 2 — letters to these people would be **informal**.

   your penfriend **your head teacher** **your mate**
   your grandma **your boss** **your MP**

Revision Summary Questions

As if the Reading part of your SATs wasn't enough, you've got to learn all this stuff about Writing as well. Oh well — it has to be done. You wouldn't think there were so many tricks to doing something as simple as writing, but trust me — making sure you know all the stuff in this section will make a huge difference to the mark you get. Don't try to bluff your way through it. Go over this section till you can answer every last one of these questions.

1) How many Writing Questions do you have to do for the exam?
2) What five things should you do as well as you can on the Writing tasks?
3) What does it mean when the task says "you should write about..."?
4) Why are story questions often harder to do than you might think?
5) For the short question, should you:
   a) use the hints you're given about what to write about
   b) ignore the hints — they're just there to catch you out?
6) When should you decide what you should say in your answer?
   a) before you start writing it, in a plan
   b) as you go along
   c) over a cup of tea at home afterwards
7) What type of answer <u>don't</u> you need a plan for?
   a) stories
   b) description pieces
   c) opinion questions
   d) ones you want to do badly on
8) When you're writing about your opinions, when should you use your strongest point?
9) How do you know what style you should write in?
10) How do you decide whether a letter is supposed to be formal or informal?
11) How do you end a formal letter when you know the name of the person you're writing to? How do you end it when you don't know their name?
12) In which type of letter should you use chatty language?
13) List a few ways you could end an informal letter.

Paragraphs

Paragraphs are a big hassle, but you get more marks for using them. Your writing is much clearer when you use paragraphs — you need to know how to use them properly.

Always Use Paragraphs

Yes, you actually get marks for writing in paragraphs. The flip side is that you lose marks if you don't. It's not enough to use paragraphs some of the time — you need to use them all the time — in stories and essays.

Paragraphs Make Things *Clear*

A paragraph is a group of sentences.
These sentences talk about the same thing, or follow on from each other.

Every new paragraph must have a space between the margin and the first word.

Leave another space every time you start a new paragraph. This shows you're writing about something different.

Leave a little gap before the first word.

When you finish the last line of the paragraph, just stop.

Start a *New Paragraph* for *Each Point* in an Essay

Paragraphs help make your essay clearer.
A new paragraph shows that you're writing about something new.

The idea that school uniforms hide the difference between rich and poor is a fantasy. Everyone can tell whose uniform came from a discount store and whose came from a designer shop.

Supporters of school uniform say that they don't want to turn school into a "fashion parade". In fact, this is exactly what they are doing when they point out the tiny ways in which a skirt or jumper doesn't quite fit the rules.

This is a new point, so start a new paragraph.

You absolutely must write in paragraphs

You've got to use paragraphs. Start a new paragraph each and every time you start a new sentence with a brand new idea, or angle, or argument. Make it clear as day to everyone — especially the examiners — that you have a shiny new point to make.

Using Paragraphs

You need to know when to start a new paragraph — you can't guess. I know it's tough, but you'll have to learn the rules. Here's a nice golden rule to start with...

Here's the **Golden Rule** for Paragraphs

Start a new paragraph every time something changes.

When you Talk about a **New Person**

Tanya looked at the scene in despair. She couldn't believe that eight soldiers could make such a mess. She sighed and started to pick up the biscuits and crisps.

A friendly face popped round the door. It was Brian. He watched Tanya grovelling around in the mess for a second or two before he spoke up.

This paragraph is about Tanya.

This paragraph is about Brian.

When Someone New **Speaks**

The same person is speaking here, so you don't need a new paragraph.

Someone new is speaking, so you need a new paragraph.

"Please don't do that on your own, Tanya," said Brian. "Come on, I'll help you clear up," he offered.

"Thanks, Brian, you're a star," replied Tanya appreciatively. "Where's everyone else? I thought there were five volunteers to clear up."

"They're all dancing over there," he explained.

Paragraphs make your work easier to read

Paragraphs make a world of difference to how good your work looks. If your writing is all in one massive chunk, it's hard to read. You have to write in paragraphs to get good marks.

Using Paragraphs

Paragraphs are great. But there's no point in knowing that if you don't know when to use them. Here are two more times when you need to start a new paragraph.

A New Paragraph for a **New Place**...

The shopping mall was utterly deserted. The uniformed security guards scratched their heads. What were they supposed to do now there was no-one to watch?

Outside Bernie's gourmet chip shop in the High Street it was a rather different story. The crowd was three deep around the shop, all pushing and shoving to get to the door. "Give us battered rat!" they clamoured. "Give us rat on a stick!".

The story has moved to the chip shop, so this is a new paragraph.

...or for a **Different Time**

This is talking about later that day.

This is talking about a long time afterwards.

At last it was over. The voice called out again, "Are you alright?" I barely had the strength to answer. Relief flooded through me in a warm, drowsy wave. Soon I would be out of the cave and home.

An hour later I was sitting in the coastguard's van, drinking hot tea from a flask. I could hear people talking all around me, but I couldn't really understand what they were saying. It was all a bit too much for me to take in. All I knew was that I was safe and everything was going to be alright.

I don't think about my ordeal that much. When I look back, it seems like something that happened to somebody else. I can't believe that I could have been so reckless.

Get into the habit of using paragraphs

Every time you change time or place in a story, a letter or an essay you have to use a new paragraph. No ifs, no buts — it's as simple as that. It's got to be second nature in the exam.

Revision Summary Questions

Well, here we are at the end of another section, and what do you know, it's time for a set of revision summary questions. Remember, the point of these is to make sure that you've learnt something from the last three pages. Go through them, and don't you dare move on to the next section until you've got them all right.

1) What is a paragraph?
2) Do paragraphs make your writing:
   a) clearer
   b) really complicated?
3) What should you do at the start of a paragraph?
4) What should you do at the end of the last line in a paragraph?
5) Do paragraphs make:
   a) not the blindest bit of difference to your mark
   b) a major difference to your mark
   c) a nice accompaniment to steak and chips?
6) What is the golden rule for starting a new paragraph?
7) What's the rule when you're writing about new people?
8) What's the rule for when people are speaking?
9) Do you need to start a new paragraph when the same person carries on speaking?
10) What's the rule for changes of place?
11) What's the rule for changes of time? (You should be spotting some kind of pattern here...)
12) The following piece of writing is really confusing.
   Turn it into a nice clear bit of writing by rewriting it with proper paragraphs:

   The biggest challenge facing Junior League Football today is the sheer number of red and yellow cards issued by referees. There is no doubt that standards of discipline have fallen sharply. Last year, 85 yellow cards and 14 red cards were issued in the first six weeks of the season. Already this year 136 yellow cards and 26 red cards have been issued. Four players are facing a four-match ban. Hector Dalrymple, chairman of the UK Federation of Under-16 Football Clubs, said last week that the situation was "reaching crisis point". Some, like Julian Fortescue of Edenhall School, disagree.
13) Write three paragraphs of a story, using the rules in this section.

Basic Punctuation

This stuff is about as basic as it gets. People do get it wrong though — when they're rushing and not thinking. Learn it really well, and you won't even need to think about it.

Don't Lose Marks for Simple Stuff

Right, now this is stuff that you already know, but it doesn't hurt to go over it again.

Every sentence starts with a capital letter, and ends with a full stop.

This is the bit you have to think about more carefully.

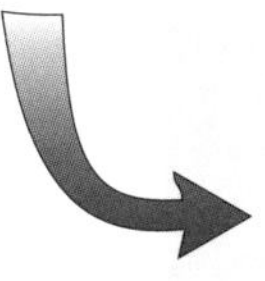

The names of people, places, organisations, days of the week and months of the year ALL NEED CAPITAL LETTERS.

Questions Need Question Marks

If a sentence is a question it's got to have a question mark. Don't forget.

Boris, can you see Mrs Marple?

Only Use One Exclamation Mark

It was absolutely amazing! I couldn't believe I was really meeting Russian pop sensation, Steppes!!!!

This makes your writing look silly, and you'll lose marks for it.

Without punctuation, your writing won't make sense

This stuff is very basic, so there's no excuse for getting it wrong. You should be able to do it without even thinking about it — that way you won't make daft mistakes.

Sentences

Everything you write has to be in proper sentences, or you're just throwing away marks.

Every Sentence Makes a ***Clear Point***

A sentence that doesn't make sense isn't much use to anyone.

> **The Golden Rule**
>
> Every sentence must make sense on its own.

Don't Let Your Sentences Run ***On and On***

Don't let your sentences run together into a huge long mess.

 *The doorbell rang it was Theo he asked if I wanted a game of five-a-side.*

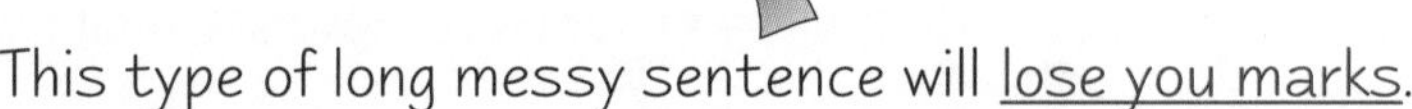

This type of long messy sentence will lose you marks.

 *The doorbell rang. It was Theo. He asked if I wanted a game of five-a-side.*

This sentence makes one point, and it's clear.

These sentences are short, but they're proper sentences.

A Sentence Has to Have a ***Verb***

For a sentence to make sense, it has to be about something. It can only be about something happening if it's got a verb. Remember, verbs are doing and being words.

Barry bought a champion racing ram. It cost £2.50.

"Cost" is the verb in this sentence.

Barry bought a champion racing ram. For £2.50.

You can't do this. There's no verb, so this isn't a sentence.

Don't write really long sentences

Working out when a sentence should end takes a little bit of thought. Keep your sentences manageable, and don't ramble. Remember this, too — no verb, no sentence.

Commas

You'll need to use commas in your Writing exam, so make sure you know how to use them.

*Use Commas to **Break Up** Sentences*

If a sentence has more than one point, a comma keeps the points separate.
Commas keep the items in lists separate, too.

I asked him to shut up, but he kept on yelling.

The comma keeps these two bits separate.

*Commas add **Extra Bits** to Sentences*

Annie and Bert, who live next door, have built a bomb shelter.

The extra bit's in the middle of this sentence. The commas go around it.

When you start a sentence with words like "Oh", "Right" or "Well", you need a comma to separate it from the rest of the sentence.

Now then, I think you need to lose that hat.
Well, I suppose you might just get away with it.

***Don't** Stick Them in **All Over** the Place*

The Mayor, Mrs Thribblewort, and the Treasurer, Mr Branchwood, said today, that the community centre would open on the 14th of September.

This comma's actually wrong — "said today" and "that the community centre..." go together — they're part of the same bit of info.

You should only put commas in when you want to break a sentence up into separate bits or when you want to stick in a bit of extra information. Randomly throwing in a bunch of commas isn't going to work.

Learn the right places to put commas in

Commas keep things apart in sentences. Make sure you use them to bracket off extra bits of information, but don't chuck them around willy-nilly. Learn the right way to use them.

Apostrophes

Apostrophes can be confusing, and cause trouble for lots of people.
You have to learn when you should use them and when you shouldn't.

*Use Apostrophes to Show **Who Owns** Something*

Kulvinder's goldfish have all died.

When it's a group of people ending in s, add an apostrophe, but no s.

I washed the judges' wigs in soy sauce.

'Men', 'women' and 'children' follow the normal rule.

The women's race was cancelled.

*Apostrophes are Used in **Short Forms** of Words*

You need apostrophes for making short forms of words — like we're instead of we are.

All of these need apostrophes. Learn them.
Don't let the easy marks slip away.

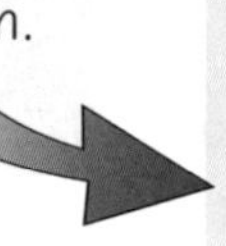

I'm	*he's*	*who's*
I'd	*won't*	*doesn't*
I've	*can't*	*here's*
we'll	*they're*	*we're*

***Its** and **It's** are Two **Different** Words*

Getting its and it's mixed up is a mistake that people make all the time.

The whale flipped its tail.

Its = belonging to it.

You don't use an apostrophe with his or hers, so don't use one with its.

It's thrown them into the air.

This is short for 'it has'.

It's a long way down, captain.

This is short for 'it is'.

Apostrophes are tricky

Remember to put in your apostrophes or you can wave goodbye to a lot of marks. You really do have to learn the stuff about its and it's. Every time you use one of them, think about it.

Speech Marks

Speech marks do just what the name says — they show when someone's speaking.
All you've got to do is use them in all the right places. You've guessed it — learn this page...

Speech Marks Show When Someone is **Speaking**

Speech marks go at the start and end of the speech.

"These aren't my shoes," said Kevin.

You need speech marks because these are the words that Kevin said.

I won't ask Mary said.

This isn't clear without the speech marks...

"I won't ask," Mary said.

You can see what's being said here.

When to Use **Speech Marks**

Be careful. You don't need speech marks if there's no one talking in your sentence.
Remember though, every time someone actually speaks in a sentence, put in speech marks.

NO SPEECH MARKS HERE

Tony said that he would lend Kevin a pair of trainers.

You don't need speech marks here.
It's not an exact quote.

SPEECH MARKS

Tony said, "I'll lend you a pair of trainers."

You use speech marks here, because
it's a direct quote — it's word for word.

Don't forget to use speech marks

You have to use speech marks when it's appropriate. See Section 3 for more about quoting.

Speech Marks

Other bits of punctuation have to fit in with speech marks, too. Learn these two rules.

*Start with a **Capital Letter***

"Don't leave the cage door open," warned Sally.

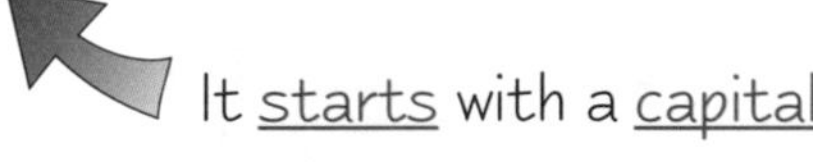

It starts with a capital letter.

Harry said, "Don't worry, I won't."

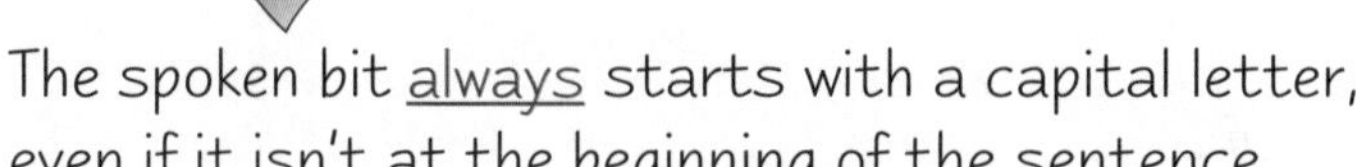

The spoken bit always starts with a capital letter, even if it isn't at the beginning of the sentence.

*End with a **Full Stop**, a **Comma** or a **Question Mark***

Ruby said, "I knew you shouldn't have trusted Harry."

The sentence is finished, so you need a full stop.

"He doesn't know if he's coming or going," she declared.

The speech has finished but the sentence hasn't. You need a comma here, not a full stop.

"Had the bear been fed before it escaped?" asked Jill.

This is a question, so here's a question mark.

Don't forget — a question needs a question mark.

Get the speech marks in the right place

Don't EVER forget to put speech marks around something that a person's actually saying. Punctuation in speech marks is a bit harder, so make sure you learn the rules.

Revision Summary Questions

You have to pay attention to all the little bitty things like full stops and apostrophes. It's a major pain, but you've got to learn all this boring punctuation. It's no good being sort of vaguely aware of it. You have to know it back to front and inside out — so that you don't make mistakes, even when you're in a hurry. You don't want to be losing marks for getting the easy bits wrong. The only way to make sure you know it all is to go over these questions until you get every single one right.

1) What's wrong with this sentence?
I've got tickets to see the raiders play the vikings on saturday.
2) What should you never do with exclamation marks?
3) What's the Golden Rule of Sentences?
4) Rewrite this as three proper sentences:
I had to find out where the sound was coming from, as I walked closer I got more and more nervous, I wanted to scream, but nothing came out of my mouth.
5) Why isn't this a sentence? *Under a palm tree with a cool drink.*
6) Are these proper sentences? If not, write a proper sentence instead:
   a) I enjoyed my holiday.
   b) The sea was warm.
   c) To the beach.
7) Put a comma in the right place to show there are two clear points here:
Before I could warn him the General sat firmly down on the broken chair.
8) Put commas in the right places to show which is the extra information:
The masked mathematician her hair streaming out behind her hurtled towards the long division sum.
9) My mate Julia doesn't bother learning punctuation. She just scatters commas through her writing and hopes for the best.
Will she:
   a) get most of them right?
   b) make a bit of a mess of it?
10) What two things do apostrophes do?
11) What's the difference between its and it's?
12) Rewrite this properly: *This food mixer is brilliant. It's slicing attachment chops vegetables really quickly. Its got a separate liquidiser for soups and milk shakes.*
13) Put speech marks into these sentence:
Earth has nothing better than a nice cosy armchair murmured Harry.
14) What's wrong with this sentence?
The masked mathematician said "next week I can show you how the equation was solved"

Use Different Words

Writing 'properly' isn't enough — your writing has to be interesting too. A good way to start making your writing more interesting is to make sure you use lots of different words.

Use *Different Words* for the *Same Thing*

English has lots of words that mean the same thing as other words. That sounds a bit pointless. But it's actually really handy. Writing is very dull if you use the same words all the time:

I went to a nice Indian restaurant last night. The waiters were nice to us and the walls were painted in a nice shade of red. I had an onion bhaji to start with and it was really nice. Then I had a nice curry. After the meal the waiters brought us mints, which was nice of them.

It may be 'correctly' written and make perfect sense, but it's really boring — the word 'nice' is in it again and again.

✔ *I went to a great Indian restaurant last night. The waiters were friendly to us and the walls were painted in a lovely shade of red. I had an onion bhaji to start with and it was really tasty. Then I had a delicious curry. After the meal the waiters brought us mints, which was good of them.*

This is loads better. It's exactly the same piece of writing except it uses lots of different words instead of "nice" — so it seems more interesting.

Vary the adjectives you use

It's easy to use adjectives like "nice" or "weird" all the time. Make sure you don't fall into this trap — you have to vary the adjectives you use to make your writing more interesting.

Use Different Words

Examiners are always impressed by a few fancy words. If you can use some in your SAT, they'll think you're really clever. And that means better marks.

Vary the **Verbs** as Well as the **Adjectives**

Look at this piece of writing. It becomes a lot more interesting just by using two new verbs instead of repeating "ran" twice.

I ran to the post box with a letter, then I ran to the shop for some chocolate. After that I ran home so I wasn't late for tea.

✔ *I ran to the post box with a letter, then I hurried to the shop for some chocolate. After that I raced home so I wasn't late for tea.*

Use different words whenever you can — they make your writing much better.

Here's another example:

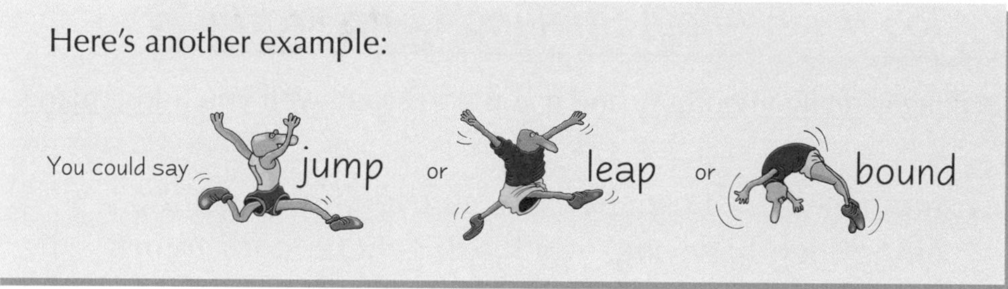

Clever Words **Impress** the Examiner

Using different words is a good start. If you can use different and clever words, you're well on the way. Long and clever words can really improve your marks.

United played badly on Saturday.  *United played lamentably on Saturday.*

The pitch was in a poor condition. 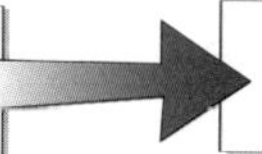 *The pitch was in an atrocious condition.*

The referee made some very stupid decisions.  *The referee made some exceedingly moronic decisions.*

Use Different Words

This page has a bit more advice on what sort of words to use, and when to use them.

*You Have to Know **When** to Use **Clever Words***

You can't use clever, long words all the time — your writing would look daft.
But you'll get extra marks if you throw them in now and then. So remember this rule:

Every now and then, try to replace a short, simple word with a long, clever one.

Of course, you have to know some clever words before you can use them in your exam. Get into the habit of looking up words you don't know in the dictionary. Chances are, the more words you know, the better you'll do.

Don't Worry** Too Much About **Spelling Long Words

1) Of course, spelling is really important, and if you don't spell well you'll lose marks. But:

   Examiners like unusual words, so even if you get the spelling slightly wrong, you'll still get credit for trying.

2) If you want to use a long word but you're not sure how to spell it, don't be afraid of getting it wrong. Give it your best go.

3) Just make sure it's the right word — don't use a word if you're not sure what it means.

   This is really the only way you can go wrong. If you try to be clever by using a long word, but get it wrong, the examiner will notice and think you're bluffing.

4) The best way to avoid this is to only use these words occasionally, instead of throwing them in all over the place.

The words you use make all the difference

You have to make your writing interesting. The first step is to use different words instead of repeating the same ones. Then throw in some long and clever words, and you're doing well.

Don't Be Boring

Here are a couple more tricks that'll help you make your writing more interesting.

Don't Use "And" and "Then" Too Much

This is something loads of people do, but it makes your writing repetitive.
It's OK to use "and" and "then" sometimes — but not too much.

I went to the beach and I put on my trunks and I walked to the sea and the water was warm and I swam for an hour.

Instead of using "and" all the time, try to use commas and full stops.

I went to the beach, put on my trunks and walked to the sea. The water was warm. I swam for an hour.

We went to the bank then we had a coffee and then we went back to the car. Then we drove to the supermarket and did some shopping, then we drove home.

Changing the word order helps you avoid using "then" all the time.

After going to the bank, we had a coffee. Then we went back to the car and drove to the supermarket. We did some shopping and drove home.

Vary the Way You Start Your Sentences

Don't start every sentence in the same way — it makes your writing dull and boring.
You'll lose marks if you do it in the SAT.

Think of different ways to start your sentences. It isn't all that hard, and it makes your writing a whole lot more interesting to read.

There was a chill in the air as Jo walked towards the house. There was nobody around. There was a big oak door and Jo knocked on it. There was a scream from inside the house.

This says the same things, but in a more interesting way.

There was a chill in the air as Jo walked towards the house. Nobody was around. Jo knocked on the big oak door. A scream came from inside the house.

Don't Be Boring

Interesting writing doesn't only use different words, it uses sentences of different lengths.

Get the **Sentence Lengths** Right

Sometimes a short sentence works best and sometimes a long one does.
Neither of them works well all of the time. It's best to use a variety of different lengths.

All short sentences:

I was walking to the station. I needed to catch a train. It left at one o'clock. I checked my watch. I was late. I decided to run. The streets were busy. I kept having to dodge people. That slowed me down. I came to a busy road. I had to wait for the green crossing sign. It seemed to take ages. Finally I crossed the road. I got to the station. The train hadn't left. It was only five to one. I looked at my watch again. It was fast.

These chunks of writing are dull, because the sentences are all short or all long.

All long sentences:

I was walking to the station because I needed to catch a train which left at one o'clock and I checked my watch and I was late so I decided to run but the streets were busy and I kept having to dodge people, which slowed me down. I came to a busy road where I had to wait for the green crossing sign and it seemed to take ages, but finally I crossed the road and got to the station where I saw the train hadn't left because it was only five to one so I looked at my watch again and it was fast.

The important thing to remember is not to write all short sentences, and not to write all long sentences. Use a mixture.

Vary the length of the sentences

The passages on this page are both dull because they don't vary the length of the sentences. The next page shows you how the passage could be made more interesting.

Don't Be Boring

The previous page showed you how boring it is when the sentences are either all long or all short. This page shows you how using a mixture makes it more interesting.

Use a **Variety** of Short and Long Sentences

This keeps the reader guessing, because they don't know what to expect next.
Here's an example of how varying the length of the sentences makes your writing better.

I was walking to the station. I needed to catch a train which left at one o'clock. I checked my watch and I was late so I decided to run, but the streets were busy and I kept having to dodge people, which slowed me down. I came to a busy road where I had to wait for the green crossing sign. It seemed to take ages. Finally I crossed the road and got to the station, where I saw the train hadn't left because it was only five to one. I looked at my watch again. It was fast.

This is more like it. The mix of long and short sentences makes this version much more interesting to read.

Ways to Make Your Writing **Better**

Here's a summary of all the stuff on the last few pages.

1) Use different words instead of repeating the same ones.
2) Use the odd clever, longer word (but not all the time).
3) Avoid using words like "and" and "then" all the time.
4) Vary the way you start your sentences.
5) Vary the length of your sentences.

Keep it interesting

It may seem like there's a lot to remember to keep your writing interesting. Just keep reminding yourself of the points in the box above, keep practising and soon it'll be second nature.

Warm-up Questions

The last six pages have some really useful tips on how to make your writing interesting. These questions will help you check you've taken it all in.

Warm-up Questions

1) Which of these words could you use to replace 'scary' and 'scared' in the story below to make it more interesting?

   panic-stricken **pants** **horrifying** **terrified** **cool** **dodgy**

   What actually happened that night was scary. I've never been so scared in my life. You'd have been scared too if you'd been there.

2) You can make your writing more interesting by including different adjectives. Name two other things you could work on to make your writing better.

3) Pick out the three sentences you think an examiner would be most impressed by.

   a) It was a really good night and the music was really good.
   b) My holiday was an exotic dream of golden beaches and gentle, blue skies.
   c) After a bone-shaking three hours, the bus gasped to a halt by a deserted-looking building.
   d) The journey was very long and we were very tired.
   e) I had never seen such a hairy, flea-bitten, pitiful mongrel in all my life.

4) How can you avoid using 'and then' all the time in your writing?

5) How important is spelling?

   a) It's not important. Just chill.
   b) It is important, but you'll get credit for other things too.
   c) It's the only thing the examiners are really bothered about.

6) How can you help yourself build up a store of effective vocabulary (good words)?

7) Which of these two versions of the same story would get higher marks and why?

   a) *She stopped. She saw nothing. Then the sounds began. The whispering and rustling and pattering sounds which suddenly surrounded her drove her further into the forest, running for her life.*

   b) *She stopped but there was nothing and then the sounds began which were whispering and rustling and pattering sounds which suddenly surrounded her and drove her further into the forest and made her run for her life.*

Adjectives

Adjectives are great for making your writing more interesting. Whenever you get a question asking you to "describe" something, make sure you cram your answer with adjectives.

Describe Things with Adjectives

Adjectives are describing words. They're a quick and easy way to spice up your writing.

Just one little adjective can completely change the impression you get from a sentence:

I ate a meal.

I ate a delicious meal.

I ate a disgusting meal.

And with three or four adjectives, you can really start to build up a picture:

I ate a delicious, sumptuous, lovingly-prepared meal.

I ate a disgusting, rancid, undercooked meal.

Adjectives Give You a Picture

Have a look at this piece of writing. It's the adjectives that really tell you what this place is like. Without them you wouldn't get much of an idea at all.

Jordios is a quiet, sleepy village on the remote island of Toonos, forty miles from Athens. Miles of unspoilt, sandy beaches stretch along the deserted coastline. The air is thick with the sweet smell of pine trees, and you can sit in the shade of the tall, elegant cypress trees that grow all over the island.

Rickety wooden fishing boats set off every morning from the small, picturesque harbour. The fishermen's faces are gnarled and sunburnt. In the evenings the locals gather in the cosy, welcoming tavernas for a friendly chat over a refreshing glass of ouzo, and a game of table top bungee jumping.

Adjectives show you're good at describing things

Adjectives are a great way of describing things effectively. If you get a question in your SAT that asks you to describe something, using plenty of adjectives is the key to getting good marks.

Comparing

You need more to describe things than just plain old adjectives.
Another good way to describe something is to compare it to something else.

Less Than, *More* Than, The *Least*, The *Most*...

Comparisons are a great way to build up a picture of something. They sound interesting and they create a big effect in your reader's mind. They're also loads of fun.

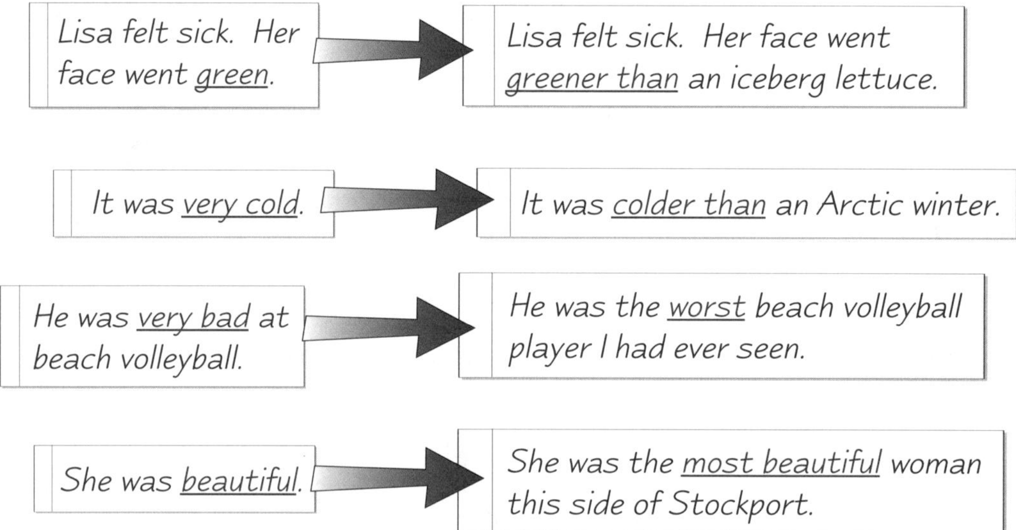

The key to making a good comparison is to pick something sensible. It's no good saying "it was colder than a pair of scissors", or "Lisa's face went as green as a doorbell".

Be Careful — *Don't* Write *"More Better"*

There's one mistake that lots of people make but which will lose you loads of marks.

When you're making a comparison, you EITHER say "more ... than" or "the most...", OR you use the form of the word that ends in "er" or "est". You don't do both.

Ted is the cleverest boy in school.

NOT the "most cleverest".

It was the most exciting time of my life.

NOT the "most excitingest".

Suzanne is prettier than her sister.

NOT "more prettier".

You're more intelligent than Einstein.

NOT "more intelligenter".

Comparisons are more useful than a Swiss Army knife

Comparisons are another great way of making your writing more interesting. But don't get confused — you either use more/most, or you use the er/est ending. Not both.

More Comparing

You don't have to use "more than" or "less than" when you're making comparisons. Another way of doing it is to say one thing is like another. That can be really effective too.

*Say that **One Thing** is **Like Another***

There are two ways of doing this.

1 The first way is to take an adjective, think of a comparison, and then instead of using "more" and "than", you use "as" and "as". You do it like this:

Beth felt as happy as a hippo in a mud pool.

That idea was as useless as a chocolate teapot.

2 The other way of saying one thing is like another is nice and simple — you use the word "like":

Her eyes lit up like the sky on bonfire night.

I'd forgotten my gloves and soon my fingers were like blocks of ice.

*You Can **Exaggerate** to Make an **Effect***

Don't worry about exaggerating when you make a comparison. That's why it's so much fun.

Jack was as tall as a tree.

Freda was as old as the hills.

Trees are generally pretty tall, and hills are pretty old, so these are good comparisons to use. You don't literally mean that Jack was as tall as a tree or Freda was as old as a hill — but people will understand.

There's nothing wrong with exaggerating

Remember the two ways to say that one thing is similar to another. It's OK to exaggerate when you make comparisons — it can make them more interesting (see page 140).

Speaking Figuratively

If you speak "literally", you mean exactly what you say.
Saying something you don't literally mean is called speaking figuratively.

Say Things you **Don't Literally Mean**

When you speak figuratively, you talk about one thing as if it's something else.
This is another way of making a comparison.

> *Bob cried so hard that a river flowed down his cheeks.*

> *Sarah needed a glass of water — there was a desert in her mouth.*

There wasn't literally a river flowing down Bob's cheeks, or a desert in Sarah's mouth. This is a clever way of saying that Bob's tears were like a river, and Sarah's mouth was as dry as a desert.

Sometimes when you speak figuratively it seems to have nothing at all to do with what you actually mean — but it's obvious when you think about it:

> *Sharon tried to delete the old files from her computer, but she wiped the entire hard drive by mistake. She had thrown the baby out with the bathwater.*

Sharon hadn't actually gone near any real babies. This is just a figurative way of saying that in the process of throwing away something she didn't need, she got rid of something very important as well.

Don't Use Too Many **Clichés**

Some figures of speech are used so often that they become boring.
They're called clichés. You hear them a lot when people are talking about sport.

> *I'm as sick as a parrot.*

> *The atmosphere's electric.*

> *It isn't over till the fat lady sings.*

You can get away with using some clichés in your SAT, but don't use too many — the examiner will think you haven't got anything original to say.

Speaking figuratively spices up your writing

Speaking figuratively is a great way to liven up your writing. Be careful, though — don't use too many clichés. It's best to be original and imaginative if you can.

Warm-up Questions

Time for another bunch of quick questions to keep you warmed up.

Warm-up Questions

1) Name two techniques which usually work well if you are asked to write a description.

2) What effect will adjectives have if you use them well?

3) Match the beginnings and endings so that these comparisons make sense.

She smiled like	*a beehive.*
It made a sound like	*a crocodile with a good dentist.*
He was as lazy as	*two trumpets and a sick donkey.*
He wore a hat which looked like	*a toad at the bottom of a well.*

4) Which of these sentences have correct grammar?

   a) It was louder than a fog horn.
   b) She was more angrier than I have ever seen her.
   c) He was the most richest man in the world.
   d) They had the cleverest dog in town.
   e) He got stranger every day.

5) Why are the sentences below *not* good comparisons?
For each one, re-write the sentence so that it's a better comparison.

   a) He went as red as a banana.
   b) It was colder than a volcano.
   c) Her voice was like an orange.

6) What happens if you exaggerate when you make a comparison?

   a) No-one will ever believe you again.
   b) You give the reader a good description that's fun to read.

7) Is this sentence meant literally or figuratively?

   His eyebrows were caterpillars asleep in the middle of his forehead.

8) True or false:
   Using clichés shows you're being imaginative.

Revision Summary Questions

So now you know loads of tricks to help you make your writing interesting. It's important that you learn all this and remember to use it in the SAT Writing Questions. Imagine you're the examiner — if you've got to read something that's dull and boring, you're not going to give it many marks. But interesting writing isn't something you can do just like that — you have to practise it so it becomes natural. Make sure you can answer all these questions, and every time you write something, try to put what you've learned into action.

1) Is using the same word all the time: a) nice b) nice c) nice d) incredibly boring?
2) Is the examiner going to be impressed by someone who can use clever words correctly?
3) Should you aim to use long and clever words:
   a) never b) all the time c) every now and then, but only when you know the meaning?
4) When you read a word and you don't know what it means, what should you do?
5) If you're in your SAT and you know a long and clever word that'd be really appropriate for something you're writing, but you're not 100% sure how to spell it, what should you do?
6) Which two words do you have to watch out for using too much?
   a) "and" and "then".
   b) "endogenous" and "exogenous".
   c) "Manchester" and "United".
7) Why is it a bad idea to start all your sentences the same way?
8) Why are adjectives great?
   a) They mean you can lie.
   b) They help you to describe something.
   c) You don't have to worry about spelling them correctly.
9) Which of these comparisons works better?
   a) It was hotter than the Sahara Desert. b) It was hotter than a piece of string.
10) Why?
11) Which of these comparisons works better?
   a) It was brighter than a candle. b) It was brighter than a million suns.
12) Why?
13) Which of these are wrong?
   a) You're weirder than me. b) She's my bestest friend.
   c) He's more intrepid than her. d) I'm the most funniest.
   e) We're the most charming. f) They're much more better.
14) What are two ways of saying that one thing is similar to another?
15) Is it OK to exaggerate when you're making comparisons?
16) What's the difference between speaking figuratively and speaking literally?
17) When is it OK to use clichés?
   a) Now and again.
   b) Most of the time.
   c) Till the cows come home.

Persuading

Sometimes you'll get a question in your SAT that asks you to write about your opinions — like in a speech or a newspaper column. That means you have to write persuasively.

Persuasive Writing is Like **Selling** Something

1) Persuasive writing is all about making someone else agree with your point of view. Trying to persuade someone to agree with you is exactly like trying to sell a product.
2) You need to sound positive and certain that you're right. If you're half-hearted and wishy-washy about what you're saying, no one is going to be convinced.
3) Make sure you've got enough good reasons to back up your opinion.
4) You'll also need some handy tricks for presenting those opinions — the next few pages will give you a few ideas.

Work Out the **Opposite** View — Then Say Why it's **Wrong**

A good way to start is to look at it from the other point of view. Think about why people might not agree with you — then you can work out how to prove them wrong.

Here's how you might plan a speech trying to persuade people to support a ban on foxhunting.

Notes: Reasons why people disagree with banning foxhunting

1. Countryside jobs — but there aren't that many

2. Need to cull foxes — but there are more humane ways

3. Tradition — but so were bear-baiting and witch-burning

These are reasons why it should not be banned.

Here's how you can say why you think these reasons are wrong.

And here's how you could write out one of those points.

Why Foxhunting Should Be Banned

Supporters of foxhunting say that it's a tradition. But in the past, it was traditional to burn witches and bait bears. Times change, and society moves on. Just because something is traditional is no reason to keep it.

Persuasive writing is about selling your point of view

Show that you've thought about what your opponents say and you still disagree with them. You'll have more chance of persuading other people that your own view is right.

Exaggerating

When you're trying to persuade people to agree with you, it's a good idea to make your own points sound even better than they are, and your opponents' points seem even worse.

Exaggerate Your Good Points

It might sound a bit unfair to exaggerate how good your own arguments are. But don't worry — everyone does it. If you don't exaggerate, people will actually think your points are weak.

This kind of thing isn't very convincing:

Global warming could be quite a problem. Some scientists think the Earth is getting warmer quite quickly. That might mean that a fair bit of farmland turns into desert, so people might not have enough food.

This one is much more persuasive:

✔ *Global warming is a massive threat to the very future of humanity. Many scientists believe the earth is getting warmer at a frightening rate. If this continues, huge areas of farmland will turn into desert, causing billions of people to starve.*

It uses strong words like "massive", "frightening" and "huge" instead of weak ones like "quite" or "a fair bit".

It says "many scientists" instead of "some".

It says "will" and "huge areas" instead of "might" and "a fair bit".

It talks about "billions of people" instead of just saying "people".

It uses the scary word "starve" instead of "not have enough food".

Be careful, though — you're allowed to exaggerate, but you're not allowed to lie. You can't say things that aren't true. If you do, people won't trust the rest of your arguments.

Make Your Opponents Sound Bad

You can also exaggerate what people who disagree say, to make them sound irrational or immoral.

Putting your opponents' point of view in your own words is a good way of making them sound bad:

Some businessmen believe we have no responsibility to the environment. They think it doesn't matter if we keep on churning out deadly greenhouse gases. All they care about is making profits.

Exaggeration can be highly effective

Exaggeration is a crucial trick for good persuasive writing. It can make you sound convincing, and make your opponents sound bad. But make sure you don't lie. That's all there is to it.

Persuasive Tricks

Here are three tricks which will make your persuasive writing a whole load better.

Talk About "*We*" and "*Us*" Whenever You Can

If you want someone to agree with you, it's a good idea to make them think they have a lot in common with you. Using the words "we" and "us" is a good way to make your audience feel like they ought to be on your side.

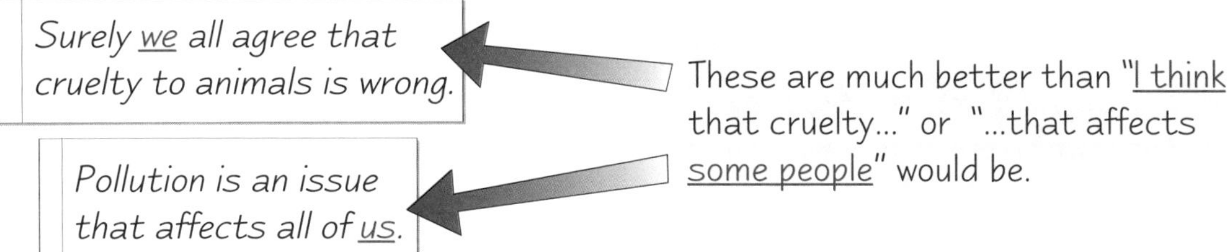

Use **Questions** to Make Your Points

Asking people something is a great way to make them sit up and take notice — even though you don't want an answer.

The trick is to say the question so that there can only be one possible answer.

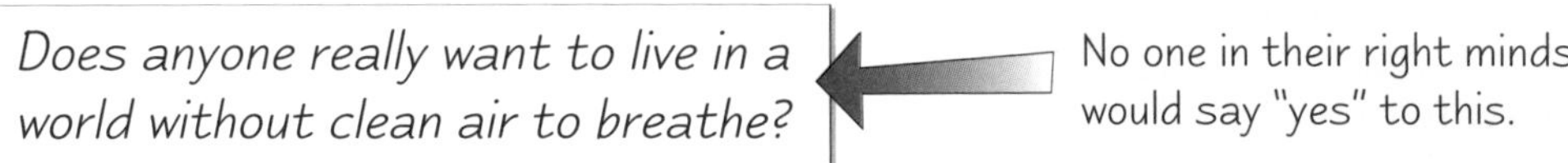

Alternatively, you can ask a question then go on to answer it yourself:

And why doesn't the government do anything about it? I'll tell you why. It's because they want big businesses to give them donations.

Use "Magic Threes" — **Three Adjectives**

Three is a magic number when you're writing persuasively. If you use three adjectives to describe something, it sounds much more effective than only using one or two.

Fossil fuels are dirty, dangerous and outdated.

Renewable energy is clean, safe and efficient.

Use these little tricks and you'll be much more persuasive

Talk about "we" and "us", use questions to make your points, and use adjectives in groups of three. These are great tricks — listen to politicians' speeches and you'll hear them all the time.

Don't Be Rude

Even if you're really convinced about something, you're not going to persuade anyone by being rude. People will only want to listen to what you say if you're polite.

Keep Your Writing Polite

If they don't agree with you, being rude to them isn't going to help. It'll just annoy them. No matter how strongly you feel about something, always be polite.

Recycling is very important. Anybody who doesn't recycle their waste is stupid and selfish.

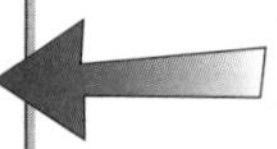
This will put people off and they'll stop listening.

Recycling is very important. It's something every one of us can do to help our planet.

People will listen to this and you might change their minds.

Keep Criticisms General and Impersonal

Don't make direct attacks on your opponents. It'll make you sound angry and aggressive, and anyone who's neutral will be turned off by your attitude — including the examiner.

If you think animal testing is acceptable, I think you're wrong.

Instead of this, say this:

It is sometimes said that animal testing is acceptable, but I think that's wrong.

Make Your Positive Points Personal

But for positive points, be as personal as you like. Using "you" gets your audience to sit up and listen, and using "we" makes them think they're on your side.

You can make a difference by not buying this company's products. Together we can bring this awful practice to an end.

This sort of personal language is especially effective when you use it as an ending.

Politeness makes your views more appealing

Always remember to be polite in your persuasive writing, and make your negative points impersonal. Being rude and aggressive offends people — and it'll lose you marks.

Warm-up and Worked Exam Questions

Warm-up Questions

1) Which of these is a lie and which is a fair enough piece of exaggeration for effect?
   a) An army of workers have to be paid to collect litter from the streets, costing the council a small fortune in wages.
   b) The council pays its workers a million pounds a week each to pick up litter from the streets.
2) Is it OK to be rude and abusive if you're writing a persuasive piece?
3) Is it a good idea to use 'you' and 'we' when you're making positive points?
4) What two reasons might you have for including a question in a piece of persuasive writing?
5) What are 'Magic Threes'? Why are they useful?

Here's an example of the sort of persuasion question you might get in your SAT, and one way of answering it (turn the page for the rest of the answer).

Worked Exam Question

This is an extract from a national newspaper report.

EATING OURSELVES TO DEATH?

Britain is facing a medical time bomb as young people opt for more and more unhealthy eating choices. They prefer to snack on junk food rather than eat balanced meals and this, doctors say, is leading to an increase in obesity, diabetes and asthma amongst our nation's schoolchildren.

What can be done to change youngsters' eating patterns?

1. Write an article for your school magazine about unhealthy eating in school. You should try to persuade other pupils to take the issue seriously, and suggest what action should be taken.

Notes

Audience — other school children

This bit's vital. Take about 15 minutes to plan. Remind yourself who it's for and why.

Purpose — persuade them it's important

Form — article

1) Intro — set scene — national problem — focus on school dinners

2) Say what's wrong — fizzy drinks, vending machines etc. — litter — poor choice of school dinners — horrible dining hall

3) Say what changes to make — change food — nicer room — more info.

4) Deal with objections — finish with need for action

Worked Exam Questions

Here's how you'd turn the plan on the previous page into a good answer.

Worked Exam Question

Starting with a question gets people to give serious thought to your ideas.

Exaggeration makes your points more forceful.

There are two comparisons here.

Use Magic Threes.

Get the readers on your side by saying 'we' and 'us'.

300 words is about the right length.

Finish by knocking down the main objection. Remember to end on a positive note.

Do you want to be unfit? No, neither do I, but from the way the newspapers carry on you'd think all young people want to do is eat themselves into an early grave. It's time to realise that the problem starts right here with the disgraceful standard of school dinners.

We all know what the problem is. The school dinners on offer are tasteless, unwholesome and usually cold. Vending machines offer unlimited supplies of crisps, chocolate and fizzy drinks and cause mountains of litter. Our dining hall is more like a railway station than somewhere to enjoy a meal. It's crowded, noisy and uncomfortable and they herd us through like cattle. It's no wonder we try not to think about what we're actually eating.

So what can we do to change the situation and save ourselves from an unhealthy future? There need to be some major changes to the quality of both the food and the eating conditions in our school. We must demand a wider range of healthy foods such as salads, fresh fruit and vegetables and vegetarian options rather than chips, burgers and more chips. We need to put pressure on our school, through the school council, to provide us with a more comfortable dining-room with better seating and more information about the food on offer. Most important of all though, we need to make healthier choices ourselves. If it's all there for us we'll have no excuse.

Some people will say that these changes will be too expensive, but surely picking up the bill for the unhealthy adults we could become will be even more expensive in the end. If we can show our school that we want to take our health seriously then perhaps our school will take us seriously and give us the school dinners that we need.

Exam Questions

Here are a couple more typical persuasion type questions. Take a good look at who their audience is supposed to be, what form they want you to write in and what they are asking you to persuade people about.

Exam Questions

1. Imagine this notice went up in your school.

> **NOTICE TO ALL STUDENTS**
>
> Following damage to classrooms during the lunch break, it has been decided that all students will be asked to leave the building during breaks and lunch times. Students may leave their belongings in classrooms which will be locked until five minutes before the start of afternoon lessons.
>
> This arrangement will apply to all year groups.

As a year 9 student, write a letter to your head teacher on behalf of your year group, persuading him or her to change this decision.

(30 marks)

2. This is an extract from a newsletter published by a local community group.

> **TIME FOR CHANGE**
>
> Our surveys last month showed up some worrying facts.
>
> - Local traffic is up by 30% on its normal daytime levels during the hours when children are going to and coming home from school.
> - There was an increase in new cases of asthma this January. Doctors say that an increase in car exhaust fumes during the winter months is partly to blame.
> - The number of children involved in road accidents around school gates and school crossings doubled last year. Our research suggests this was due to congestion caused by parents picking up and dropping off their children in cars, which cuts down how far people can see when crossing the road.

You are asked to write the speech to give at your school's open evening. Your speech is to try to persuade parents and their children to use family cars less for journeys to and from school, and to walk and cycle to school more often.

(30 marks)

Revision Summary Questions

This is the last section about the Writing part of your SAT, and the last section of the whole book. If you've learned everything in the book so far, you'll have learned all the skills you need to get through the SAT. But before you can say that, you have to make sure you know this section properly. It's well worth it because chances are you'll get a question in the SAT that wants you to write persuasively — whether it's a speech, a magazine article or a letter. And persuasive writing is something you can get really good at just by learning the tricks in these pages.

1) What should you do after you have listed the reasons why people might disagree with you?
2) How can you make your opponents' beliefs sound crazy?
3) Which of these is a good use of exaggeration?
   a) "The arms industry causes some suffering in the world."
   b) "The arms industry is directly responsible for causing untold misery to millions."
   c) "The arms industry likes to kidnap newborn babies and roast them on a spit."
   What is wrong with the other two sentences?
4) Is it a good idea to tell lies about your opponents?
5) Why is it a good idea to use "we" and "us" a lot in persuasive writing?
6) Which of these would be a good question to use in a piece of persuasive writing?
   a) "What is the capital of Estonia?"
   b) "Would you like your children to grow up in a world without wild flowers?"
   c) "Do you think pollution could possibly be a bit of a problem?"
   What makes it such an effective question?
7) What's the other good trick to use with questions?
8) Is the idea of using three adjectives to describe something:
   a) OK but not very useful?
   b) pointless and strange?
   c) clever, valuable and effective?
9) What would you write to try to convince someone who thinks that you should be rude in persuasive writing that it's better to be polite?
   a) "Don't be idiotic, you pea-brained fool, that idea stinks."
   b) "Many people find that being polite works much better."
10) Why is it a good idea to keep your criticisms general and impersonal?
11) Can your positive points be personal?
12) What is an especially effective time to use personal language?
   a) As an ending.
   b) When you're exaggerating.
   c) When asking to borrow a fiver.

Practice Exam Instructions

1) Just like in the real exams, there are **three papers** that you have to do:
   - the Reading Paper (pages 147-156)
   - the Writing Paper (pages 157-160)
   - the Shakespeare Paper (pages 161-165)
2) Each paper is a **separate test**. You don't have to do all three papers in one go.
3) Read the **instructions** on the **first page of the paper**, before starting to answer the questions.
4) Mark your answers using the **mark scheme** on pages 179-185.
5) The **Shakespeare Question** in this practice exam is about *Macbeth*. If you're not studying *Macbeth*, then pick an exam question about your play from Section 4 or 5 and do that instead.

English

EY STAGE

3

EVELS

4-7

RACTICE PAPER

Reading

CGP

Key Stage 3

English Test

Reading Paper
Heat Sensitive

Instructions

- Before you start to write, you have **15 minutes** to read the Reading Booklet.
- From that point you will have **1 hour** to write your answers.
- Try to answer **all** of the questions.
- There are **13** questions, worth **32** marks.
- Check through all of your work carefully before the end of the test.
- If you're not sure what to do, ask your teacher.

First Name ____________________

Last Name ____________________

School ____________________

Moving Up

This is a short story about a boy who is about to leave his primary school and go to secondary school.

Long before the bell was due to ring that day, David could feel himself bursting to be free of his regulation grey school shirt. His shorts had been sewn at the back more than once by his mother, who'd said, "David, you're moving up at the end of this term and I'm not getting you new shorts just for six weeks." After the end of this week he would never have to wear them again and soon his mother would be buying him a pair of long, black trousers to match his new blazer and school tie ready for September.

He could not think too much of this yet. The familiar classroom buzzed in the heat around him and the sun showed the chalk dust floating in front of the blackboard. His teacher moved slowly and heavily between the groups of tables checking his classmates' sums with a bright red pen. She had no need to check his, but she would anyway. His sums were never wrong and week after week he was times-table champion. Only Ben Michaels had knocked him off the top once before and that was the day the scab had come off his knee and he couldn't concentrate properly because it was itching. He didn't mind too much. They were best friends and they sometimes used to play in the mud in each other's gardens until one of their mothers said, "We don't buy you clothes to roll around the floor in. Get up and get washed and don't let me catch you at it again." Now they only scuffed the edges of the dusty patches with the soles of their shoes and rubbed them clean in the grass before going into the house. Last summer he wouldn't have cared what the mothers said, but this year he knew he was growing up. Rolling in the mud suddenly seemed a bit embarrassing, a bit childish for someone about to move up.

He'd heard that expression many times now. "David, you're moving up soon, you'll be a young adult then," was his father's favourite comment at the moment, but he had no idea what it really meant. One sticky day in June, his class had been to the big school. It was huge and he'd been scared of getting lost. He hadn't enjoyed the day. Suddenly he was so much smaller than everyone else.

David turned his attention back to the stuffy air of the classroom and wondered if the hands on the clock had stopped. He thought about the times-tables championships and hoped they would still have them when he moved up. He yawned, feeling bored. He wanted his teacher to gather them all upon the carpet in front of the big desk and tell them a magical story before the end of the day. Instead, she continued to check sums. He had to be content with staring at the frogspawn in the fish tank which he had helped to collect from the pond the week before.

He felt so hot and the air was so still. He glanced towards Ben Michaels to see what he was doing and he noticed straight away the bright coloured paper poking out from underneath his sum book. Ben Michaels was the best in the class at doing things he shouldn't — he never got caught. David could remember last year when he had glued all of Mrs Fitzgerald's pencils into the stand and she couldn't get them out when the inspector came. He couldn't imagine what Ben Michaels was doing under his sum book but he knew it was something he shouldn't.

Suddenly David noticed his teacher walking towards him. "David Donaldson," he heard her begin, "you're day dreaming." He could have told her word for word what she would say next: "You're moving up soon and you won't get away with it then." David looked at her as she bent over to mark his sums. He didn't want to move up. He wanted to go to school here in the sunshine forever with the class that he had always known.

Cider with Rosie

This is an extract from Laurie Lee's autobiography. In this extract he remembers his arrival in the village his family have just moved to.

I was set down from the carrier's cart at the age of three; and there with a sense of bewilderment and terror my life in the village began.

The June grass, amongst which I stood, was taller than I was, and I wept. I had never been so close to grass before. It towered above me and all around me, each blade tattooed with tiger-skins of sunlight. It was knife-edged, dark, and a wicked green, thick as a forest and alive with grasshoppers that chirped and chattered and leapt through the air like monkeys.

I was lost and didn't know where to move. A tropic heat oozed up from the ground, rank with sharp odours of roots and nettles. Snow-clouds of elder-blossom banked in the sky, showering upon me the fumes and flakes of their sweet and giddy suffocation. High overhead ran frenzied larks, screaming, as though the sky was tearing apart.

For the first time in my life I was out of the sight of humans. For the first time in my life I was alone in a world whose behaviour I could neither predict nor fathom: a world of birds that squealed, of plants that stank, of insects that sprang about without warning. I was lost and did not expect to be found again. I put back my head and howled, and the sun hit me smartly on the face, like a bully.

From this daylight nightmare I was awakened, as from many another, by the appearance of my sisters. They came scrambling and calling up the steep rough bank, and parting the long grass found me. Faces of rose, familiar, living; huge shining faces hung up like shields between me and the sky; faces with grins and white teeth (some broken) to be conjured up like genii with a howl, brushing off terror with their broad scoldings and affection. They leaned over me – one, two, three – their mouths smeared with red currants and their hands dripping with juice.

"There, there, it's all right, don't you wail any more. Come down 'ome and we'll stuff you with currants."

And Marjorie, the eldest, lifted me into her long brown hair, and ran me jogging down the path and through the steep rose-filled garden, and set me down on the cottage doorstep, which was our home, though I couldn't believe it.

That was the day we came to the village, in the summer of the last year of the First World War. To a cottage that stood in a half-acre of garden on a steep bank above a lake; a cottage with three floors and a cellar and a treasure in the walls, with a pump and apple trees, syringa* and strawberries, rooks in the chimneys, frogs in the cellar, mushrooms on the ceiling, and all for three and sixpence a week.

I don't know where I lived before then. My life began on the carrier's cart which brought me up the long slow hills to the village, and dumped me in the high grass, and lost me. I had ridden wrapped up in a Union Jack to protect me from the sun, and when I rolled out of it, and stood piping loud among the buzzing jungle of that summer bank, then, I feel, was I born. And to all the rest of us, the whole family of eight, it was the beginning of a life.

But on that first day we were all lost. Chaos was come in cartloads of furniture, and I crawled the kitchen floor through forests of upturned chair-legs and crystal fields of glass. We were washed up in a new land, and began to spread out searching its springs and treasures. The currants were at their prime, clusters of red, black, and yellow berries all tangled up with wild roses. Here was bounty the girls had never known before, and they darted squawking from bush to bush, clawing the fruit like sparrows.

Our Mother too was distracted from duty, seduced by the rich wilderness of the garden so long abandoned. All day she trotted to and fro, flushed and garrulous **, pouring flowers into every pot and jug she could find on the kitchen floor. Flowers from the garden, daisies from the bank, cow-parsley, grasses, ferns, and leaves – they flooded in armfuls through the cottage door until its dim interior seemed entirely possessed by the world outside – a still green pool flooding with honeyed tides of summer.

I sat on the floor on a raft of muddles and gazed through the green window which was full of rising garden. I saw the long black stockings of the girls, gaping with white flesh, kicking among the currant bushes. Every so often one of them would dart into the kitchen, cram my great mouth with handfuls of squashed berries, and run out again. And the more I got, the more I called for more. It was like feeding a fat young cuckoo.

* A type of plant.
** Talkative, chatty.

Summer Temperatures Soar

This is an article that appeared in a newspaper during the summer.

Weather experts warned yesterday of temperatures higher than those of the notorious summer of 1976. The next week will be crucial in breaking British records if the forecasters have got it right. As workers left their offices in central London and other cities around Britain early yesterday due to heat exhaustion, doctors warned would-be sunbathers to apply the highest factor cream available and to drink more than the usual eight glasses of water a day.

Recent days have seen temperatures around Britain at their highest for many years, and researchers have been flocking to hot-spots in places as unlikely as Aberdeen and the Outer Hebrides in a rush to be the first to measure the highest temperature since records began. So far, temperatures have remained tantalisingly short of the record, but scientists are confident they will be waving their thermometers with glee before the end of this week. Three separate thermometers at the nearest University's research centre must confirm temperatures before they are accepted as official by the Met. Office.

Meanwhile, a spokesperson for the Environment Agency issued a statement asking people to be sensible about their domestic water consumption, reminding the public that reservoirs are draining almost dry with several weeks of summer still left to run. Hosepipe bans are already in place throughout most of the country and farmers are feeling the impact, with crops reported to be failing through dehydration. Livestock is being kept in the shade of barns and many farmers are reported to be worried about their next step in the event of the heatwave continuing.

The Minister for Education has asked all primary school headteachers to consider sending pupils home each day at lunchtime until temperatures subside so that they do not become overheated in ill-ventilated classrooms. Exam boards are worried that the heat will affect the public examinations going on over the next week and have asked schools to do all they can to provide comfortable working conditions for students.

Questions 1-5 are about 'Moving Up' (page 148-9)

1. Between lines 1 and 10 we find out about the atmosphere in the classroom. Pick out two quotations and explain how they help the reader imagine the atmosphere in the classroom.

Quote	How it creates atmosphere

(4 marks) 4 marks

2. Between lines 26 and 32 pick out **two** things that suggest David is quite young.

....

....

(2 marks) 2 marks

3. From lines 33 to 39 pick out **one** thing that you think shows how David feels about Ben. Explain your answer.

....

....

....

(2 marks) 2 marks

4. Describe how David feels in lines 40 to 44 and explain how you know this.

....

....

....

(2 marks) 2 marks

5. Look at the whole extract. What impression do you get of what David is like?

....

....

....

....

....

....

(3 marks) 3 marks

Questions 6-9 are about 'Cider with Rosie' (page 150-1)

(page 150-1)

6. In the first sentence choose and write down TWO words that show the narrator's feelings about arriving in the village.

....

(1 mark) 1 mark

7. From lines 3-16 pick out **two** phrases that the author has used to show the narrator's fear.

....

....

(2 marks) 2 marks

8. From lines 29-33 what impression do you get of the cottage they have moved into?

....

....

....

....

(2 marks) 2 marks

9. From lines 17-23, pick out **two** phrases that create an impression of the narrator's feelings for his sisters.

....

....

(2 marks) 2 marks

Questions 10-13 are about 'Summer Temperatures Soar' (page 152)

10. Between lines 1-6 pick out **two** words or phrases that show people think the heat needs to be taken seriously.

....

(1 mark) 1 mark

11. From lines 7-14 explain how scientists feel about the possibility of a record high temperature.

....

....

....

....

(2 marks) 2 marks

12. From lines 15-27 pick out and explain **two** facts in the article which might concern the reader.

What the article says	How this might concern the reader

(4 marks) 4 marks

Question 13 is about 'Moving Up' and 'Cider with Rosie'

13. 'Cider With Rosie' and 'Moving Up' are both about boys moving into a new phase of their life. Explain how the two texts help us to imagine the boys' experiences and feelings. You should write about:

- the language the authors use
- how you react to the texts
- any similarities and differences between the texts.

(5 marks)

5 marks

English

EY STAGE
3

EVELS
4-7

RACTICE PAPER
Writing

Key Stage 3

English Test

Writing Paper

Instructions

- This paper is **1 hour and 15 minutes** long.
- You should spend about:
  45 minutes on Section A
  30 minutes on Section B
- Section A, the longer writing task, is worth 30 marks.
- Section B, the shorter writing task, is worth 20 marks.
- You have 15 minutes for planning your answer to Section A, using the planning grid provided.
- Check through all of your work carefully before the end of the test.
- If you're not sure what to do, ask your teacher.

First Name ______________________

Last Name ______________________

School ______________________

Section A

Longer writing task

Website Advertisement

This is a memo to the publicity department of the Internet company 'LastMinuteHotels.com'.

> Hi Folks!
>
> This fantastic hotel in Benidorm has just come onto our books — and it needs to go on the website straightaway. Please can you write it up so that it sounds really good? We need to get it booked up as soon as possible.
>
> The hotel's got the following going for it:
> - two pools, a sauna and a gym
> - nightly entertainment
> - three bars
> - family-friendly restaurant
> - king-size beds
> - across the road from the beach
> - five minute flat walk into the town centre
>
> Put in loads of detail to hook the customers — sun, sandy beaches, palm trees... you know the stuff. Also try and make it sound ideal for everyone — from old age pensioners to teenage ravers. It's a tricky job but I'm sure you're up to it.
>
> Cheers,
> Mike

Write the advertisement for this hotel to go on the company's website.

(30 marks)

Longer writing task

Planning page

You can use this page to plan your work. (This page will not be marked.)

- Words and phrases to open the advertisement

- Descriptive details to make the hotel sound as good as possible

- Details to make it appeal to a wide audience

Section B

Shorter writing task

The Haunted Castle

Imagine you are a newspaper reporter who has been asked to write an article about a group of people who believe in ghosts. You go with the group to spend the night in a haunted castle.

The editor of the newspaper sends you this note:

> I think you should be able to write a really good article about your night in the haunted castle.
>
> Remember to write about what the castle was like, what happened when you were there and how you felt.
>
> Oh, and say whether you believed in ghosts before you went and whether you do now!

Write the article for the newspaper about the night you spent at the haunted castle.

You **do not** need to set it out like a newspaper article.

(20 marks including 4 for spelling)

English

KEY STAGE
3

LEVELS
4-7

PRACTICE PAPER
Shakespeare

Key Stage 3

English Test

Shakespeare Paper
The Tempest

Instructions

- This test is **45 minutes** long.
- It tests your reading and understanding of *The Tempest* and is worth 18 marks.
- Check through all of your work carefully before the end of the test.
- If you're not sure what to do, ask your teacher.

First Name ______________________________

Last Name ______________________________

School ______________________________

The Tempest

Act 1, Scene 2, lines 5-32

Act 5, Scene 1, lines 1-96

Explain how Prospero's character is portrayed as both powerful and kind in these scenes.

Support your ideas with references to the extracts printed on the following pages.

(18 marks)

The Tempest

Act 1, Scene 2, lines 5 to 32

In this extract, Miranda is worried when she sees a ship caught in the storm that Prospero has created.

MIRANDA O, I have suffered
With those that I saw suffer! A brave vessel,
Who had no doubt some noble creature in her,
Dashed all to pieces! O, the cry did knock
Against my very heart! Poor souls, they perished.
Had I been any god of power, I would
Have sunk the sea within the earth or ere
It should the good ship so have swallowed and
The fraughting souls within her.

PROSPERO Be collected.
No more amazement. Tell your piteous heart
There's no harm done.

MIRANDA O, woe the day!

PROSPERO No harm.
I have done nothing but in care of thee,
Of thee, my dear one, thee, my daughter, who
Art ignorant of what thou art, nought knowing
Of whence I am, nor that I am more better
Than Prospero, master of a full poor cell,
And thy no greater father.

MIRANDA More to know
Did never meddle with my thoughts.

PROSPERO 'Tis time
I should inform thee farther. Lend thy hand,
And pluck my magic garment from me. So,
(lays down his mantle)
Lie there my art. Wipe thou thine eyes. Have comfort.
The direful spectacle of the wreck, which touched
The very virtue of compassion in thee,
I have with such provision in mine art
So safely ordered that there is no soul —
No, not so much perdition as an hair,
Betid to any creature in the vessel
Which thou heard'st cry, which thou saw'st sink.

Act 5 Scene 1, lines 1 to 96

In this extract, Prospero prepares to talk to the people who betrayed him in the past.

Enter PROSPERO *in his magic robes, and* ARIEL

PROSPERO Now does my project gather to a head.
My charms crack not, my spirits obey, and time
Goes upright with his carriage. How's the day?

ARIEL On the sixth hour, at which time, my lord,
You said our work should cease.

PROSPERO I did say so,
When first I raised the tempest. Say, my spirit,
How fares the King and 's followers?

ARIEL Confined together
In the same fashion as you gave in charge,
Just as you left them — all prisoners, sir,
In the line-grove which weather-fends your cell.
They cannot budge till your release. The King,
His brother, and yours, abide all three distracted,
And the remainder mourning over them,
Brim full of sorrow and dismay, but chiefly
Him you termed, sir, 'the good old lord, Gonzalo'.
His tears run down his beard, like winter's drops
From eaves of reeds. Your charm so strongly works 'em
That if you now beheld them your affections
Would become tender.

PROSPERO Dost thou think so, spirit?

ARIEL Mine would, sir, were I human.

PROSPERO And mine shall.
Hast thou, which art but air, a touch, a feeling
Of their afflictions, and shall not myself,
One of their kind, that relish all as sharply,
Passion as they, be kindlier moved than thou art?
Though with their high wrongs I am struck to th' quick,
Yet with my nobler reason 'gainst my fury
Do I take part. The rarer action is
In virtue than in vengeance. They being penitent,
The sole drift of my purpose doth extend
Not a frown further. Go release them, Ariel.
My charms I'll break, their senses I'll restore,
And they shall be themselves.

ARIEL I'll fetch them, sir.

Exit

PROSPERO *(drawing a magic circle on the ground)*
Ye elves of hills, brooks, standing lakes, and groves;
And ye that on the sands with printless foot
Do chase the ebbing Neptune, and do fly him
When he comes back; you demi-puppets that
By moonshine do the green sour ringlets make,
Whereof the ewe not bites; and you whose pastime
Is to make midnight mushrooms, that rejoice
To hear the solemn curfew; by whose aid —
Weak masters though ye be — I have bedimmed
The noontide sun, called forth the mutinous winds,
And 'twixt the green sea and the azured vault
Set roaring war. To the dread rattling thunder
Have I given fire, and rifted Jove's stout oak
With his own bolt; the strong-based promontory
Have I made shake, and by the spurs plucked up

The pine and cedar. Graves at my command
Have waked their sleepers, oped, and let 'em forth,
By my so potent art. But this rough magic
I here abjure, and, when I have required
Some heavenly music — which even now I do —
To work mine end upon their senses that
This airy charm is for, I'll break my staff,
Bury it certain fathoms in the earth,
And deeper than did ever plummet sound
I'll drown my book.

Solemn music. Here enters ARIEL *before, then* ALONSO*, with a frantic gesture, attended by* GONZALO, SEBASTIAN *and* ANTONIO *in like manner, attended by* ADRIAN *and* FRANCISCO. *They all enter the circle which* PROSPERO *had made, and there stand charmed, which* PROSPERO *observing, speaks:*

A solemn air, and the best comforter
To an unsettled fancy, cure thy brains,
Now useless, boiled within thy skull. There stand,
For you are spell-stopped.
Holy Gonzalo, honourable man,
Mine eyes, ev'n sociable to the show of thine,
Fall fellowly drops. The charm dissolves apace,
And as the morning steals upon the night,
Melting the darkness, so their rising senses
Begin to chase the ignorant fumes that mantle
Their clearer reason. O good Gonzalo,
My true preserver, and a loyal sir
To him thou follow'st! I will pay thy graces
Home both in word and deed. Most cruelly
Didst thou, Alonso, use me and my daughter.
Thy brother was a furtherer in the act. —
Thou art pinched for't now, Sebastian. — Flesh and blood,
You, brother mine, that entertained ambition,
Expelled remorse and nature, who, with Sebastian —
Whose inward pinches therefore are most strong —
Would here have killed your king, I do forgive thee,
Unnatural though thou art. Their understanding
Begins to swell, and the approaching tide
Will shortly fill the reasonable shore
That now lies foul and muddy. Not one of them
That yet looks on me, or would know me. Ariel,
Fetch me the hat and rapier in my cell.

Exit ARIEL *and returns immediately*

I will discase me, and myself present
As I was sometime Milan. Quickly, spirit
Thou shalt ere long be free.

ARIEL *(sings and helps to attire him)*
Where the bee sucks, there suck I;
In a cowslip's bell I lie;
There I couch when owls do cry.
On the bat's back I do fly
After summer merrily.
Merrily, merrily shall I live now
Under the blossom that hangs on the bough.

PROSPERO Why, that's my dainty Ariel! I shall miss thee;
But yet thou shalt have freedom.

Page 6 — Warm-up Questions

1) The correct answer is **b**.
2) The statement is **false**.
3) a) Disgust.
   b) He shows his temper by kicking the cat as he leaves.
4) b) "The writer creates a feeling of tension by…" is the way to start your answer.

Page 9 — Exam Questions

1) One reason is that the ship was believed to be "unsinkable" so no-one thought the lifeboats would be needed.
   Another reason is that putting more lifeboats on board would have taken up valuable deck space.
   [1 mark for each point. Maximum of 2 marks.]
2) The phrase "basking in the elegance" describes the wealthy passengers and "packed into steerage" describes the poor ones.
   [1 mark for each phrase. Maximum 2 marks.]
3) The tearing of calico (a kind of cloth) would be quite a quiet sound. This means the collision was not very loud and so at first nobody thought anything important had happened.
   [2 marks for full explanation.]
4) a) The simile is "clinging in clusters or bunches, like swarming bees". [1 mark]
   b) Any reasonable answer — for example:
   The simile helps the reader to imagine the scene more vividly — that there were still great numbers of people on the ship, clustered in groups. [1 mark]

Page 16 — Warm-up Questions

1) The number of marks and the amount of space they give you to write in.
2) Go on to some other short questions and come back to the mini-essay later. Tackling the short questions can help you get your ideas together and collect marks at the same time.
3) **b** is correct. Think of the list they give as a bit of free help. It shows you where to start.
4) Underline key words in the question. Look for instruction words like 'write down' and 'explain'. Also look for words which point to the subject of the question such as 'What impression...' and 'How is suspense created...'
   You can also underline the bits of text which will help you answer the question.
5) **a**, **b** and **d** are correct. Most of the questions asking you 'how' a writer does something just want you to comment on some or all of these three areas.

Page 19 — Exam Questions

1) The room is bare, with little furniture.
   It is dark because the broken window panes have been covered with paper.
   The room is very dirty, with writing and cuts on the desk and stained walls.
   The room is uncared for. No-one has bothered to paint or repair it. *(Other answers are possible.)*
   [1 mark for each point. Maximum of 2 marks.]
2) Two possible phrases are "endurance of cruelty and neglect" and "the scowl of sullen suffering".
   (Other answers are possible.)
   [1 mark for each phrase. Maximum of 2 marks.]
3) To get the full five marks you need to cover all three pointers.
   • *the kind of details he includes* — You could mention how ugly the room is with its broken windows and damaged desks. The boys are described as having "haggard faces" and "stunted growth".
   • *the words he uses* — There are lots of negative things listed which you could mention — "ugliness", "cruelty", "suffering", "helplessness" and "neglect". There's also the sarcastic tone of the writer when he calls the boys "noblemen". Explain how these words give a very negative impression of the school.
   • *the length of the sentences* — Write about the use of very long sentences to put in long lists of awful details about the school.

Page 26 — Warm-up Questions

1) Statements **c**, **d** and **e** are true.

Page 29 — Exam Questions

1) Any reasonable answer, e.g. "Remember my first night?" or "'Course you do." [1 mark]
2) Any reasonable answer — for example:
   To create a vivid picture of how bad life is on the streets and therefore engage the reader's sympathy for Link. [2 marks]
3) Any reasonable answer — for example:
   It provides a first-hand viewpoint about how bad living on the streets is. This backs up the report's argument that running away is dangerous for young people.
   [2 marks]
4) To get the full 5 marks, you need to refer to the question and to each of the prompts — remembering to support your points with quotes and examples.
   - *the dangers involved* — Talk about how each text highlights the dangers involved in living on the streets, e.g. you could mention the 'Scouser' who attacked Link during his first night on the streets in 'Stone Cold'. Mention the statistics quoted in the University of York press release, e.g. that one in eight young people who ran away were physically hurt — this is effective because it's a shockingly high proportion.
   - *the views of both writers* — Discuss how both writers believe that living on the streets is dangerous, e.g. in 'Stone Cold' the writer uses a first person narrator — this is effective because it lets us see life from the teenager's point of view, gaining our sympathy. The University of York press release uses statistics from an "extensive" study to highlight the dangers, making the article sound accurate and reliable.
   - *the language used in the texts* — Refer to both writers' use of language and say how this is effective in showing us the dangers. E.g. you could write about how 'Stone Cold' uses informal language to engage the reader's interest, such as "dosser" and "dosh", or how he uses short sentences to create tension and suggest danger. For the University of York Press Release, you could write about the formal language and how this is effective in making the topic seem serious and important, e.g. "the findings of the most extensive study".

Page 41 — Warm-up Questions

1) Stick to the paragraphs they've told you to look in and include quotes in your answers on the longer questions.
2) The word "sneer" tells us that Charlie doesn't think much of the gift.
3) The correct order is: **c, b, d, a**.

Page 45 — Exam Questions

1) "Passed listlessly" [1 mark]
2) He thought Hallward was just being nice because they are friends. [1 mark]
3) Because Dorian hasn't said anything / is silent. [1 mark]
4) Any two appropriate phrases, e.g. "A mist of tears", "the delicate fibre of his nature", "he felt as if a hand of ice had been laid upon his heart." [1 mark for each phrase. Maximum of 2 marks.]
5) You need to cover all the prompts to get the full five marks.
   - *his reaction to the picture* — You could mention how delighted Dorian is at how beautiful he looks — "a look of joy came into his eyes". When he first sees the picture, he stands "motionless", and hardly hears what Hallward is saying to him — this shows that he has become completely taken in by the beauty of the picture.
   - *his thoughts about getting older* — You can tell he hates the idea of ageing, as all the words he uses to describe it are negative, e.g. "wrinkled", "deformed", "hideous". The thought of it clearly depresses him — he feels "a sharp pang of pain", and starts crying, even though he's still young and attractive at the moment. This shows how important his appearance is to him.
   - *what he says in the final paragraph* — By now he's clearly become obsessed with maintaining his youthful looks, as ageing is all he can talk about. He says that there's "nothing in the whole world" that he wouldn't give to avoid looking old. You could also mention that there's an excited tone of voice in this speech, suggesting he is becoming irrational.

Page 47 — Exam Questions

1) There are seven big forests still "intact". [1 mark]
2) "Stop talking! Act now!" [1 mark]
3) a) The trees are used for plywood boards and wood pulp (for everyday products). [1 mark]
   b) The writer wants us to think it is wrong to use trees so big ("giant") and old ("thousands of years old") for such ordinary things. [1 mark]
4) The writer is implying that politicians haven't been doing their jobs properly. It says we need to "remind" politicians of their "promises and responsibilities". [2 marks for the point backed up with quote]

5) To get the full five marks for this question make sure you cover all the prompts in your answer.
   • *the first and last paragraphs* — Talk about how the writer encourages you to feel part of something big by saying "all over the world". You could mention how "Ancient Forests Ambassador" sounds like an important job title or mention the repetition of "you can too" in the first and last paragraphs.
   • *the use of dates and statistics* — There are lots of possibilities here. Whichever ones you choose, remember to say what effect they have on us. You could mention that 80% of the original forests have already been destroyed, showing how severe the situation is, or that more than 15 different countries are involved with the Kids for Forests campaign, so it's a worldwide issue. Paragraph 5 says 35,000 kids have been involved in the past and 240,000 people have signed petitions, so it seems like it can't be that hard to get involved. There's also the deadline — politicians promised to stop species dying off by 2010 but they haven't even started yet, and this gives a sense of urgency to the campaign.
   • *the writer's choice of language* — You could write about the slogan ("Stop Talking! Act now!") which motivates people to take action, or the way the writer says "we" all the time, which makes the reader feel involved.

Page 54 — Warm Up Questions

1) That's right, the odd one out is bribes. The only way to get those marks is by giving plenty of reasons, examples, quotes and explanations to back up your points.
2) You always use speech marks ("...") to show that you have taken words directly from the text.
3) This one was a trick question of course. It doesn't matter which order you put these in as long as you include them all. It's probably easiest to start with your point first, but there are no definite rules.
4) Some good advice would be to keep quotes short — even quoting a single word is fine. Try to back up your points with quotes as often as possible. A little and often is the guide.

Page 56 — Exam Questions

1) The writer repeats the word "dark", giving the impression of a gloomy atmosphere. The house also seems neglected and uncared for because of the dust on the corridor floor.
   Or similar answer. [2 marks for full description]
2) It seems that Frank can't quite believe his luck when the snake ignores him. His amazement is shown by two strong words to describe the snake going past — "incredibly, miraculously". [2 marks for full explanation]
3) There are quite a few points you could make to answer this question. To get the full five marks, you will need to back up each point with references to the text, either in your own words or with direct quotes. Here's a sample answer:
   In the first sentence we are told that Frank is so frightened he can't move. It is as if he wants to but his fear is too powerful — he's "paralysed with fright". The writer tells us directly what he is feeling. He experiences a "thrill of terror". "Terror" is a very extreme word and it sounds as though the feeling came upon him suddenly.
   Both these ideas are repeated in the phrase "horrified, transfixed" to describe Frank as the snake gets closer. This makes him seem helpless and unable to escape. When the danger seems to have passed Frank is left shaking and sweating. This shows how tense he was.

Page 64 — Warm-up Questions

1) Try to read your set scenes as often as you can. The more you read them, the easier they'll be to understand.
2) No. As long as you know what's going on and you can work out how the characters are feeling you'll be fine.
3) a) There are five acts in a Shakespeare play.
   b) A new scene usually starts when some time has passed or the story moves to a different place.
4) **a** is the correct answer.
5) Sometimes there will be stage directions to explain how a character says their lines, but usually you can work it out from what they're saying and who they're with, and your knowledge of the character's personality.

Page 64 — Exam Questions

1) For 18 marks, cover both scenes and include a quotation or example to back up each point you make.
   A good answer would make at least three points about each scene. Here are some suggestions.
   Act 1, Scene 2 — You could write about Caliban appears bad-tempered and aggressive. For example, he puts elaborate curses on Prospero: "A south-west blow on ye / And blister you all o'er". You could also write about how Caliban seems very bitter about how he has been treated by Prospero: "This island's mine, by Sycorax my mother, / Which thou tak'st from me." You could also discuss how Caliban has no guilt about trying to rape Miranda in the past: "O ho, o ho! Would't had been done." This shows a very nasty side to his character.
   Act 3, Scene 2 — You could write about Caliban's violent desires in this scene. He encourages Stephano to kill Prospero: "There thou mayst brain him". You could also write about how Caliban is quite cunning; he promises that Stephano can have Miranda, if he kills Propsero: "She will become thy bed, I warrant". You could also write about how Caliban is very happy at the idea of Prospero being killed: "Thou mak'st me merry. I am full of pleasure." This shows an evil side of his character.

We also get a glimpse of his sensitive side: "sounds and sweet airs, that give delight, and hurt not".

Page 65 — Exam Questions

2) For 18 marks, cover both scenes and include a quotation or example to back up each point you make. A good answer would make at least three points about each scene.
Act 2, Scene 1 — You could write about how Antonio tries to persuade Sebastian that they should kill Alonso and Gonzalo. Antonio seems the stronger character and he leads Sebastian into supporting his plan, for example saying: "Then tell me, / Who's the next heir of Naples?" You could write about how Antonio claims to have no conscience: "Ay, sir, where lies that?" You also write about how Antonio lies very quickly and easily when Alonso and Gonzalo wake up to see him with his sword drawn: "O, 'twas a din to fright a monster's ear".
Act 3, Scene 3 — You could write about how Antonio whispers about his murderous plans to Sebastian in front of the people he wants to kill, for example: "(aside to Sebastian) Let it be tonight". This shows he is arrogant and confident. You could also write about how Prospero describes Antonio and Sebastian as "worse than devils" which emphasises to the audience that they are evil characters. You could say that Antonio expresses gladness that Alonso thinks his son has drowned: "I am right glad that he's so out of hope". This shows that Antonio is only concerned about his own power and wealth not other people's lives or emotions.

3) For 18 marks, cover both scenes and include a quotation or example to back up each point you make. A good answer would make at least three points about each scene. Here are some suggestions:
Act 1, Scene 2 — You could write about the way Prospero seems quite manipulative, for example he interferes in Ferdinand and Miranda's romance: "this swift business / I must uneasy make". You could say that Prospero seems a protective father of Miranda — he feels that Ferdinand should prove his love "lest too light winning / Make the prize light." You could also write about the way that Prospero is willing to be nasty to achieve his aims, for example he pretends to make Ferdinand his slave, "Come! / I'll manacle thy neck and feet together."
Act 5, Scene 1 — You could write about the way that Prospero values Gonzalo's friendship, saying "noble friend, / Let me embrace thine age". He seems loyal to people who have treated him kindly. You could also write about the way that Prospero forgives his brother Antonio for betraying him, ("I do forgive / Thy rankest fault") which shows a kinder side to Prospero's character. You could talk about how Prospero is powerful and manipulative in this scene, holding back the information that Ferdinand is alive from his father Alonso.

4) For 18 marks, cover both scenes and include a quotation or example to back up each point you make. A good answer would make at least three points about each scene. Here are some suggestions:
Act 1, Scene 2 — You could write about how Ariel is Prospero's servant. At the beginning of this scene, Ariel is very obedient and seeks Prospero's favour. For example, he addresses him as "great master" and describes how he has carried out Prospero's orders in every detail. You could write about how Prospero expects Ariel to work very hard for him. When Ariel comes back from organising the tempest, Prospero says "there's more work" for him. You could write about the conflict between Prospero and Ariel. Ariel wants his freedom in return for "worthy service", but Prospero feels he hasn't worked hard enough for it yet. You could discuss the change in Prospero when Ariel brings up the issue of freedom. Prospero changes from being friendly to Ariel and calling him "My brave spirit!" to being angry and calling him a "malignant thing". Prospero makes it clear that he is in charge, and Ariel reacts by giving in to him, saying "Pardon, master. / I will be correspondent to command".
Act 5, Scene 1 — You could write about how Prospero bosses Ariel around because he is his servant, for example: "Ariel, / Fetch me the hat and rapier in my cell." In this scene, Prospero holds out the prospect of freedom as a way of motivating Ariel to do everything he asks: "Quickly, spirit / Thou shalt ere long be free." You could write about how Ariel seems happy that his moment of freedom is getting closer, and how he is willing to be obedient to Prospero in the expectation that he will soon be freed. For example, he sings as he goes about his work ("Merrily, merrily shall I live now / Under the blossom that hangs on the bough") which shows his happiness. You could mention that Prospero seems to have affection for Ariel: "Why, that's my dainty Ariel! I shall miss thee."

Page 66 — Exam Questions

5) For the full 18 marks you need to make at least three good points, backed up with quotations and comments or explanations. It's really good if you can comment on particular words and phrases and how they affect you/the audience.
Act 3, Scene 5 — You could write about how Richard is very deceitful; he tells Buckingham to act a part when he says "As if thou were distraught and mad with terror", to convince the mayor that they have been attacked. He acts frightened and says "Look back! Defend thee, here are enemies!" You could also write about how Richard pretends that he is upset — "So dear I lov'd the man that I must weep", even though the audience know that he ordered the innocent Hastings' death.
Richard is also very convincing. He convinces the mayor that Hastings had to die for "The peace of England, and our persons' safety". You could mention how Richard manages to convince people to crown him King by pretending he doesn't want to be the King.
Act 5, Scene 4 — You could write about how brave Richard is in this scene. Catesby says he "enacts more wonders than a man" — in other words he's a superhuman fighter, and he's not afraid to fight his enemies face to face. You could write about how he doesn't retreat even though they're in danger of losing; "Rescue, fair lord, or else the day is lost!" You could also mention how his horse is killed from under him, yet he still wants to go on fighting; "A horse! A horse! My kingdom for a horse!"

6) For the full 18 marks, go through both scenes and find some examples, explaining how the characters react to the dreams. As always, you've got to write about both scenes if you want the full 18 marks. Choose quotations from each scene and explain what they show. Look for three points to make about each scene.

Act 1, Scene 4 — Clarence has a dream that Richard pushes him off a ship and he felt "what pain it was to drown". This makes him really frightened as he thought he'd died and gone "Unto the kingdom of perpetual night". The audience can tell how deeply it affects him as the language is so powerful — "mock'd the dead bones", "the tempest to my soul". The dream makes Clarence feel that he's going to get what he deserves, and he just wants to protect his family from the same fate, as he begs "execute Thy wrath in me alone".

Act 5, Scene 3 — Richard and Richmond dream about the same ghosts the night before the battle, but it means different things to each of them. E.g. the ghost of Prince Edward appears and tells Richard "despair therefore, and die" but tells Richmond "the wronged souls / Of butcher'd princes fight in thy behalf". So the ghosts in the dream seem to tell Richard and Richmond what the outcome of the battle will be. His dreams make Richard more afraid of losing than guilty about what he has done; "I'll play the eavesdropper, / To see if any mean to shrink from me". Richard accepts that the world will see him as a bad person: "And every tale condemns me for a villain". He is shaken and upset by the dreams: "Cold, fearful drops stand on my trembling flesh". The dreams also make him realise how alone he is: "There is no creature loves me".

7) For 18 marks, cover both scenes and include a quotation or example to back up each point you make. A good answer would make at least three points about each scene.

Act I, Scene 2 — Anne rejects Richard but he says that her eyes have 'drawn salt tears' from him, even though he never usually cries. Shakespeare also uses dramatic language — Richard offers Anne his sword to stab him and bares his chest; "I lay it naked to the deadly stroke". This is a very dramatic way to ask for forgiveness. Richard says he killed Anne's husband and father-in-law, but "twas thy heavenly face that set me on". This makes it surprising that he manages to convince her. Shakespeare keeps up the suspense with short lines of dialogue as Anne starts to give in, saying that his heart and his words are "false". Richard's replies "Then never was man true" — he appears to be saying that no one could be more truthful about this than he is, but he could also be saying that all men lie to women. Richard tells direct lies here: "my poor heart", "thy poor devoted servant" and "my repentant tears". Richard gives Anne a ring at the end, and she believes that he has "become so penitent" that she agrees to meet him again.

Act 3, Scene 7 — Richard acts modestly and declines to become King — "Your love deserves my thanks, but my desert / Unmeritable shuns your high request." He speaks about his "poverty of spirit", although the audience knows that he has evil ambition. He even proposes that the young Prince Edward should be King; "The royal tree hath left us royal fruit". Richard has told Buckingham to say that Edward is illegitimate — they're both acting parts. Richard is adamant that he won't be King; "I cannot, nor I will not, yield to you", and eventually accepts "against my conscience and my soul". This is almost funny, as Shakespeare makes Richard act so differently from his true character.

Page 67 — Exam Questions

8) There are 18 marks for this question. To get them all you will need to find things to say about Beatrice and Hero from both scenes, backing them up with quotes and detailed comments. Once again, you should aim to make at least three points about each scene.

Act 2, Scene 1 — You could point out that one of the things we notice immediately is that Beatrice has far more to say than Hero — compare their comments on Don John. Beatrice jokes with Leonato about not wanting to marry but says Hero has a duty to do as she's told. Compare the way they talk to their masked partners too. Hero and Don Pedro are very polite and well spoken — Beatrice's conversation is far more aggressive. You should quote examples to demonstrate this.

Act 4, Scene 1 — Hero reacts to Claudio's accusations with shock and confusion. She doesn't say much and faints. She seems unable to defend herself and says "Oh God defend me! How I am beset!" You could point out that Beatrice is much more energetic in defending Hero. She is shocked too but stands up for Hero and persuades Benedick to challenge Claudio on her behalf. She's angry that she isn't a man — she'd like to kill Claudio herself.

9) For 18 marks you'll need to write about both scenes. Make three good points about each one and back them up with quotes and comments.

Act 2, Scene 1 — You could explain that the atmosphere here is relaxed — Leonato is teasing Beatrice and she's enjoying shocking everyone with her views on men and marriage, e.g. "Would it not grieve a woman to be over-mastered with a piece of valiant dust?". The masked dance adds fun to the scene and even Antonio joins in the banter. We see lots of characters enjoying themselves. The noble characters speak in prose in this scene to give a less serious atmosphere.

Act 5, Scene 1 — Explain that here the characters indicate the serious atmosphere by speaking in verse. Antonio sets the tone at the start by saying "If you go on thus, you will kill yourself." Leonato says this advice is "as profitless / As water in a sieve" — he's inconsolable, creating a desperate and miserable mood. Leonato and Claudio start arguing, and Antonio wants to fight Claudio — "I'll whip you from your foining fence!" — so the atmosphere is tense and violent.

10) You will get the full 18 marks for writing in detail about both brothers, backed up with examples taken from both scenes. Remember to comment on your quotes and examples. Try to find three good points for each scene.

Act 1, Scene 1 — You could say that Don Pedro first arrives as a victorious commander. Leonato's welcome speech shows how popular Don Pedro is. He calls Leonato "my dear friend". He can joke easily with the others but also has a serious conversation with his close friend Claudio and offers to help him win Hero. By contrast, Don John says hardly anything except to admit, "I am not of many words".

Act 1, Scene 3 — Here Don John tells us more about himself. Comments such as "I am a plain-dealing villain" show he doesn't mind being disliked. Conrade tells us Don Pedro has been good to Don John, but Don John is still bitter because he lost the battle. Don John resents Claudio too, e.g. he says, "If I can cross him any way, I bless myself every way," so he's clearly a very hateful man.

Page 76 — Warm-up Questions

1) Shakespeare wrote his plays about 400 years ago.
2) **c** is correct. The lines will make more sense if you follow the punctuation. Remember — the end of a line doesn't mean the end of a sentence.
3) a) Talking in poetry sounds posher.
   b) A common person would speak in poetry if they were speaking of grand ideas, or trying to be clever. This is often a source of comedy.
4) Riddles, comparisons, rhymes and rhythm are all features of Shakespeare's writing, and the kind of things you might end up commenting on in your exam. You'll probably spot some funny looking spellings too. Language has changed a lot in 400 years.
5) Some characters have funny looking names, either because they are from foreign countries or because Shakespeare wants us to laugh at them, e.g. Dogberry. Some of the things they do can also seem strange. Shakespeare's world was quite different to our world today and ways of behaving have changed.

Page 76 — Exam Questions

1) Write about both scenes for the full 18 marks and back up your points with quotes and explanations.
   Aim for three points about each scene.

   Act 1, Scene 1 — The men chat about women in this scene, e.g. Don Pedro says, "I shall see thee, ere I die, look pale with love", showing that they're comfortable enough to tease each other. Claudio trusts Benedick enough to talk about loving Hero in front of him and Benedick is very relaxed when the others accuse him of pretending to be a woman-hater. They are all very open with each other, e.g. Don Pedro says "I speak my thought."

   Act 5, Scene 1 — In this scene, things have changed. Beatrice has made Benedick promise to kill Claudio in revenge for what he's done to Hero. Benedick says a lot less in this scene — he is colder and refuses to join in any jokes. When Claudio says they have been looking for him to cheer them up with his wit he says, "It is in my scabbard — shall I draw it?" When Benedick says to Claudio, "You are a villain. I jest not," they don't take him seriously at first. You could also comment on their reaction when they realise he means it, which shows the split between them.

Page 77 — Exam Questions

2) For the full 18 marks, mention both scenes in your answer and include quotations and comments to back up your points.

   Act 1, Scene 1 — You could start by saying that the first time Beatrice speaks in the play it is to ask about Benedick, but she calls him "Signor Mountanto", and mocks him before he even arrives. You could write about the way they insult each other, e.g. Benedick's first words to Beatrice are, "What, my dear Lady Disdain — Are you yet living?" They seem to enjoy the chance to show off their wit. Benedick says, "I would my horse had the speed of your tongue". Talking is an important part of their relationship.

   Act 5, Scene 2 — When Beatrice enters, Benedick can't think how to reply to her banter and he seems uncomfortable. He says, "Thou and I are too wise to woo peaceably," creating a strange sense that they're both in love and at war at the same time. You could mention that Benedick is being more open about his feelings at this point: "I love thee against my will". You could point out that Beatrice asks Benedick if he's coming to Leonato's house with her to find out the news about Hero, showing that by this stage she finds it hard to disguise the fact that she wants to be with him: "Will you come presently?"
3) Your answer needs to make points about both scenes for the full 18 marks and you will need to include quotations and explanations too.

   Act 2, Scene 3 — Claudio and Don Pedro speak deliberately loudly and their comments are funny because they are so exaggerated. Write about how they build in insults too — for example when Claudio says Beatrice is wise Don Pedro says "In everything but loving Benedick". You could also explain the comic effects of Benedick's lines which show he's been taken in, e.g. he says, "This can be no trick", but that's exactly what it is. Your answer could include a comment on how unusually politely Benedick speaks to Beatrice at the end of the scene.

   Act 3, Scene 1 — Hero's remarks about Beatrice are funny because we know Beatrice is hiding and can hear what she's saying, e.g. "Disdain and scorn ride sparkling in her eyes." Explain the comic effect of them suddenly changing the subject as they leave. You could also quote from Beatrice's speech which shows how shocked she is, e.g. "Stand I condemned for pride and scorn so much?"
4) If you want all 18 marks you will have to refer to both scenes and use quotations and comments to back up your points.

   Act 2, Scene 1 — You could comment on how Don John and Borachio only have to say a few words to convince Claudio that Don Pedro has betrayed him and Claudio says "'Tis certain so, the prince woos for himself". You could find quotes to show his extreme reaction before Benedick arrives. He sounds sulky when he says "I wish him joy of her" and he is like that with Don Pedro too at first. Benedick makes him seem ridiculous when he says "Alas poor hurt fowl! Now will he creep into sedges."

Act 4, Scene 1 — Your answer could comment on how much more serious his anger is at the church. He says of Hero, "Her blush is guiltiness, not modesty," which shows a harsh and bitter side to his character. He humiliates Hero in public and seems more concerned about his own public image than with finding out the truth, which makes him seem superficial and quick to judge. Quote some of the insults he pours on Hero, e.g. "this rotten orange", and explain that this badly affects our opinion of him too.

Page 78 — Exam Questions

5) For the full 18 marks you need to make three good points about each scene, backed up with quotations and comments or explanations. It's really important to comment on particular words and phrases and how they show different aspects of the two characters.

Act 3, Scene 1 — You could write about how Buckingham is plotting alongside Richard. He instructs Catesby to "sound thou Lord Hastings / How he doth stand affected to our purpose". Richard sends very friendly messages to Hastings; "Commend me to Lord William", but he shows his true character when he says "Chop off his head". He doesn't try to hide much of his plotting from Buckingham, and offers him an incentive to stay loyal to him — "when I am king, claim thou of me / The earldom of Hereford". Richard appears to treat Buckingham as a friend, as he says "look to have it yielded with all kindness".

Act 4, Scene 2 — You could write about how Richard is very gracious to Buckingham at the start; "by thy advice / And thy assistance is King Richard seated." But he makes no attempt to hide his feelings when he asks him to kill the young princes; "I wish the bastards dead". Buckingham asks for "some pause" before he replies, suggesting that there are some crimes that he won't commit. Richard's attitude to Buckingham changes as soon as Buckingham hesitates, and he says that he "No more shall be the neighbour to my counsels". This shows Richard is a strong character — he won't accept anyone disagreeing with him, or being slow to support him. When Buckingham asks Richard to keep the promise made in Act 3, Richard repeatedly ignores him and eventually says "I am not in the giving vein today". Buckingham's surprise that such a cunning and evil person doesn't keep promises shows that he is quite naive; "Repays he my deep service / With such contempt?".

6) For the full 18 marks you will need to cover what happens in both scenes. Aim to focus on three key bits of language from each scene that emphasise the atmosphere of evil.

Act 3, Scene 4 — You could write about how it's obvious that Richard is laying a trap for Hastings, when he says "devilish plots" and then encourages Hastings to say that such people "deserved death" — this is quite an evil trap. You could write about the strength of the language Richard uses, such as "blasted sapling", and calling Hastings "protector of this damned strumpet". You could also mention how Hastings realises there were evil omens and how he's a victim of Margaret's evil "heavy curse". You could also mention the violent words he uses, like "slaughter house" and "butchered".

Act 4, Scene 2 — You could write about the way that Richard initially hints about killing the young princes, then just comes out and says "I wish the bastards dead". You could mention how Buckingham's formal response contrasts with Richard's anger and suggests that he's overstepped the mark; "Your Grace may do your pleasure". The arrangement to pay murderers to do it seems very evil; "whom corrupting gold / Will tempt unto a close exploit of death?" You could also mention the danger that Buckingham might be in for refusing; "stops he now for breath! Well, be it so."

7) For the full 18 marks you need to make three good points about each scene, backed up with quotations and comments or explanations.

Act 3, Scene 4 — You could mention that Richard finds out that Hastings said he wouldn't support Richard's claim to the throne: "he will lose his head ere give consent". You could also mention how Richard is hiding his feelings from Hastings; Hastings says "by his face straight shall you know his heart", as he still believes that Richard likes him. The way that Richard makes Hastings fall into a trap and condemn himself shows his cunning; "tell me what they deserve". You could also mention how quickly he turns on Hastings: "Off with his head!" and the way he shows his temper here — he wants it done immediately: "I will not dine until I see the same". The reference to making Richard late for dinner seems to emphasise how cruel he is: "the Duke would be at dinner".

Act 4, Scene 2 — You could write about how Richard shows his evil character here — "O bitter consequence, / that Edward still should live". You could mention how Richard shows his anger in a gesture when Buckingham doesn't immediately agree to the murder of the young princes; "he gnaws his lip". You could mention how the lines "stops he now for breath! Well, be it so" might have a double meaning; now Buckingham has hesitated to obey, Richard will 'stop his breath' permanently by having him killed. You could mention how ruthless and cunning his plans are to be rid of his wife, Anne, and marry his niece: "Rumour it abroad / That Anne my wife is very grievous sick". Richard also ignores Buckingham's requests by refusing to honour his promise; "I am not in the giving vein today", showing how Buckingham is no longer in his favour.

Page 79 — Exam Questions

8) For 18 marks, cover both scenes and include a quotation or example to back up each point you make.
A good answer would make at least three points about each scene. Here are some suggestions:
Act 2, Scene 1 — You could write about the evilness of Antonio's character. When he claims to have no conscience: "Ay, sir, where lies that?" it creates a threatening atmosphere. You could write about how Antonio gradually persuades Sebastian to kill Alonso. At first he drops hints about his plan: "What might, / Worthy Sebastian — O, what might!", then the tension rises as he makes his plan clear by saying "Whom I with this obedient steel, three inches of it, / Can lay to bed for ever". You could also talk about the dramatic irony used, when Antonio encourages Alonso to go to sleep saying, "We two, my lord, / Will guard your person while you take your rest, / And watch your safety". It soon becomes clear that Antonio doesn't have Alonso's safety in mind at all — instead he intends to kill him.
Act 3, Scene 2 — You could write about the gruesome words Caliban uses to describe how he wants Prospero to be killed: "There thou mayst brain him" and "Batter his skull, or paunch him with a stake, / Or cut his wezand with thy knife". The violence and malice of these descriptions creates a threatening atmosphere. You could also talk about the threat that they will try to abduct Miranda when they kill Prospero: "And that most deeply to consider is / The beauty of his daughter". You could write about Ariel's presence as a spirit, frightening Stephano and Trinculo by playing music.

9) For the full 18 marks you need to make three good points about each scene, backed up with quotations and comments or explanations.
Act 3, Scene 3 — You could write about the reactions of Alonso and Gonzalo to the spirits bringing the banquet: "What harmony is this?" and "Marvellous sweet music!". The characters are amazed by the magic and this creates a sense of wonder. You could also write about the stage directions which are very dramatic and surreal: "Enter Ariel, like a harpy, claps his wings upon the table". You could mention the way that Ariel describes his own magical powers: "My fellow-ministers / Are like invulnerable". You could write about the references to mythical beasts. Alonso says that having seen the spirits he could now believe in "unicorns" and the "phoenix".
Act 4, Scene 1 — You could write about how the spirits put on a performance, creating a magical atmosphere. For example, one of them arrives on a flying chariot drawn by peacocks. You could write about the references to Roman and Greek mythology, with the spirits taking the form of classical goddesses like Juno and Ceres. You could also write about the poetic language and song which help to create a magical atmosphere, for example: "You nymphs, called Naiads, of the windring brooks, / With your sedged crowns and ever harmless looks". You could also mention Ferdinand's reaction: "This is a most majestic vision".

10) For 18 marks, cover both parts of the scene and include a quotation or example to back up each point you make.
A good answer would make at least three points about each extract. Here are some suggestions:
Act 2, Scene 1 (lines 104-137) — You could write about how Sebastian is very insensitive when he talks to Alonso. Alonso is distressed and fears that his son has died. Sebastian says that it is Alonso's fault that his son has died, "Sir, you may thank yourself for this great loss" because it was Alonso's decision to marry his daughter to someone in Africa and undertake the voyage. You could write about how Sebastian doesn't stop when Alonso says "Prithee peace". Instead he carries on blaming Alonso for everything which has happened, showing an insensitive and cruel side to his character. You could write about how Gonzalo criticises Sebastian, saying, "You rub the sore, / When you should bring the plaster." This emphasises to the audience how unkind Sebastian is being.
Act 2, Scene 1 (lines 197-312) — You could write about how Sebastian is persuaded into the plot to kill Alonso by Antonio. Antonio starts by dropping hints to Sebastian: "What might, / Worthy Sebastian — O, what might!" before gradually revealing his plan. Sebastian quickly agrees to the plan. This makes Sebastian appear a weak character who is easily led. You could write about how Sebastian appears greedy for money and power. Antonio tempts him to replace his brother Alonso, by saying how much richer he is since he took over from Prospero: "look how well my garments sit upon me, / Much feater than before." You could also write about how Sebastian lies easily when Alonso and Gonzalo wake up to him with his sword drawn. He claims he heard "a hollow burst of bellowing / Like bulls, or rather lions". This shows that he is deceitful and untrustworthy.

Page 86 — Warm-up Questions

1) Any three of the following:
   - Read through both scenes
   - Underline the keywords in the question
   - Work out what the question is asking you to do
   - Underline words/phrases in the extracts that you could use
   - Make a plan of what points you are going to make and the order you are going to make them in.
2) You will get more marks. One out of every three marks is given for a quote.
3) You should plan your answer because it will help you get your ideas straight, you can arrange your points into a sensible order and it will help you not leave out anything important.
4) You should spend about 10 minutes reading and planning.
5) Shakespeare gives us an idea of what a character is like through what they say, how they say it, what they say about each other and what they do.

Page 88 — Exam Questions

1) For the full 18 marks you need to make six good points each backed up with a quote and an explanation.
Act 1, Scene 1 — You could write about how Richard tells the audience that he's bad, when he says "I am determined to prove a villain" at the beginning of the play. We could admire him for being honest to the audience. We can admire the way he lies to Clarence, saying "I will deliver you, or else lie for you". When Richard says "lie for you" Clarence thinks he means 'take your place' but Richard means 'tell lies', as he has arranged for Clarence to be executed.
Act 3, Scene 7 — Richard is so clever in this scene that you have to admire him. He pretends that he doesn't know that he is going to be crowned King, even though he's arranged it all, as he says "I do suspect I have done some offence". He even pretends to be offended by what Buckingham is saying, as he says "I cannot tell if to depart in silence / Or bitterly to speak in your reproof". You could also mention how he points out that the young Prince Edward should rule; "royal fruit", which then gives Buckingham the chance to say that they're illegitimate.
2) For the full 18 marks make three good points about each prompt — each backed up with a quote and explanation.
Here are some suggestions:
• *How the characters' feelings towards each other change* — Discuss how at the start of the play, Benedick and Beatrice are always arguing and putting each other down. E.g. in Act 1 Scene 1 Benedick calls Beatrice "Lady Disdain" and Beatrice says, "nobody marks you." Discuss how as the play goes on, Beatrice and Benedick are both tricked into believing that the other is in love with them. They become more and more friendly until finally the trick is revealed and they decide to get married.
• *The language the characters use when they speak to each other* — Talk about how at the beginning of the play, the language they use is spiteful and insulting, e.g. Benedick comments: "Well, you are a rare parrot-teacher" and Beatrice replies: "A bird of my tongue is better than a beast of yours." In Act 4 Scene 1, though, their language is very different — more tender and gentle. E.g. Benedick shows his concern when he says "Lady Beatrice, have you wept all this while?" Beatrice is also much sweeter, e.g. "I love you with so much of my heart that none is left to protest."
3) For 18 marks, cover both scenes and include a quotation or example to back up each point you make.
A good answer would make at least three points about each scene. Here are some suggestions:
Act 1, Scene 2 — You could write about how Miranda is naive and innocent having led a sheltered life on the island. For example, she says that Ferdinand is only "the third man that e'er I saw, the first / That e'er I sighed for". You could also write about how she falls in love quickly with Ferdinand on their first meeting. This shows she's romantic and impressed by good looks: "There's nothing ill can dwell in such a temple". You could write about how Miranda is quite brave in speaking in defence of Ferdinand when her father pretends to hate him. For example, after Prospero has called her a "foolish wench" for liking Ferdinand, she answers back "I have no ambition / To see a goodlier man".
Act 3, Scene 1 — You could write about how Miranda is very passionate and serious in her love for Ferdinand; for example she asks him straight out: "Do you love me?". You could also write about how she proposes to Ferdinand, which is quite a confident and risky thing to do considering how short a time they have known each other: "I am your wife, if you will marry me". You could write about how Miranda's innocent, sheltered life is also emphasised in this extract, for example she says: "I do not know / One of my sex, no woman's face remember".

Page 94 — Warm-up Questions

1) For a question about directing a scene you would need to write about these things:
• the way the actors move and say their lines
• their appearance — clothes, props and make-up
• lighting and sound to show the mood
2) False. You need to understand what the characters are saying if you are going to make their feelings clear to an audience.
3) **b** is the right answer.
4) Shakespeare uses lots of tricks in his characters' persuasive speeches — one of the most common is using comparisons.

Page 96 — Exam Questions

1) For the full 18 marks you'll need to discuss both scenes in detail. Try to write about three places in each scene where you would make decisions as a director and explain what effect you want them to have. Remember to quote some lines and explain why they are important.
Act 1, Scene 2 — You could talk about how Prospero says the line "No, wench — it eats and sleeps and hath such senses / As we have". He could say this in a patronising and sarcastic tone of voice to Miranda because she is so innocent she doesn't realise that Ferdinand is a man. You could talk about how Prospero acts when he makes his asides to the audience. For example, when he says "*(aside)* They are both in either's pow'rs, but this swift business / I must uneasy make", he could turn to face the audience and talk in a whisper as if he is confiding his private thoughts. You could talk about how Prospero acts when he pretends to dislike Ferdinand. When Prospero says, "he's a traitor. Come! / I'll manacle thy neck and feet together", he could shout the lines and grab Ferdinand by the back of the neck to pull him away from Miranda.
Act 5, Scene 1 — You could write about how Prospero acts when he draws the "magic circle" on the ground. He could stand still and just move one finger to create the circle. This would help create a magical atmosphere. You could write about how he says the line "Graves at my command / Have waked their sleepers, oped, and let 'em forth". He could say this in a whisper to

make the audience feel frightened. You could also write about how Prospero acts when the other characters are standing in the magic circle "charmed". Prospero could walk around the outside of the circle, looking into the faces of the different characters as he talks about them. For example, he could stand next to Gonzalo and perhaps put a hand on his shoulder as he says "O good Gonzalo, / My true preserver". You could explain how his actions need to make it clear to the audience that he is in control.

2) For the full 18 marks you need to make six good points, backed up with quotations and explanations.
Even though it's a question about directing, you still have to comment on particular words and phrases and how you would use them to create an effect on the audience.

Act 1, Scene 1 — You have to explain why you think these directions are appropriate, and what effect you hope to have on the audience. You could say that Richard is meant to be deformed, and his evil, dishonest character is meant to show in his physical appearance. You could instruct the actor to limp onto the stage, and to stand hunched up on the stage. At the beginning of Richard's soliloquy you could have him sounding upbeat but in a sarcastic way, maybe changing the tone of his voice when he's talking about the contrasts; "dreadful marches to delightful measures". Then you could tell him to change his tone to a more angry one, and move nearer the audience from the point when he says "But I, that am not shap'd for sportive tricks". He could look over his shoulder before he says "I am determined to prove a villain", as if he's checking that he's not being overheard. He could adopt a confiding tone with the audience, as if he's letting them in to his secrets. He should also look pleased when he says "should Clarence closely be mew'd up".

Act 3, Scene 7 — You could tell the actor to sound very reluctant to be King, and yet obviously be acting a part. He could do this by overacting his denial a little bit, especially on lines like "my desert / Unmeritable shuns your high request." He could also sigh a little as he says "so much is my poverty of spirit" and perhaps turn his eyes upwards as if he's looking up at heaven. He could even look absolutely horrified that anyone would think of making him King instead — "God defend that I should wring from him", and when he says "O, do not swear". Then his attitude could get more business-like when he says "Call them again." He should speak more quickly, yet still be acting a part. He should make the audience very aware of the double meaning in lines 226-234, and perhaps even turn towards them a little as he says "For God doth know, and you may partly see". He could put his hands together in prayer when he says "let us to our holy work again".

3) For the full 18 marks you'll need to discuss both scenes in detail. Try to write about three places in each scene where you would make decisions as a director and explain what effect you want them to have. Remember to quote some lines and explain why they are important.

Act 4, Scene 1 — Talk about how the scene seems to be a happy one until the mood changes. Write about how you'd show Leonato's jollity and Hero's happiness. Quote lines which show how confident they both are. You could bring out Claudio's hidden anger and then aggression through his tone of voice and movements. You would also want to focus on how shocked and confused Leonato and Hero become, e.g. when Hero says "Is my lord well, that he doth speak so wide?"

Act 5, Scene 4 — Claudio doesn't realise he's about to marry Hero. Comment on how he'd show his grim determination to go through with the wedding whoever the bride is, e.g. "I'll hold my mind were she an Ethiope". Your directions should show how everyone moves and speaks in a serious way at first and how this could change when Hero is revealed. Focus on when Hero first speaks to Claudio and how he reacts. You could also write about the tension that is still there between Benedick and Don Pedro in lines 40 to 51 — you could show this tension by having them standing face-to-face, saying their lines in a deliberate, pointed way.

Page 100 — Warm-up Questions

1) **b** and **c** are good pieces of advice for writing about themes.
2) **b** and **c** are good pieces of advice about quotes.

Page 101 — Exam Questions

1) To get all 18 marks you'll need to focus on both scenes, and make about three points for each one. Remember to put quotes in.

Act 3, Scene 4 — You could comment on how Margaret teases Hero about her gown and the wedding night, and Hero's shocked reaction to that, e.g. "art not ashamed?" which shows that she cares about her reputation. You might want to comment on the banter between Beatrice and Margaret; "A maid, and stuffed!", that shows how girls were expected to be virgins when they got married, or they would lose their reputation.

Act 4, Scene 1 — You could mention how Claudio says that Hero is "but the sign and semblance of her honour" — she appears virtuous but really she's a "rotten orange". You could also mention how both Claudio and Don Pedro feel that their reputations have been damaged by agreeing to the marriage; "I stand dishonoured". Also, Don Pedro says "upon mine honour" when he wants to swear that something is true. You could also mention how Leonato feels that he has been dishonoured by his daughter — "smirched thus and mired with infamy". Her reputation is so damaged by the accusation that he'd rather that she was dead, and she's brought shame on him too.

2) For all 18 marks make about three points for each scene.

Act 2, Scene 2 — You could write about how Don John just wants to "cross" the marriage to get at Claudio. You could mention how Borachio is proud of his own dishonesty and ability to trick people, when he says "so covertly that no dishonesty shall appear in me". You could also mention how Borachio tells Don John to "intend a kind of zeal both to the Prince and Claudio" as if he was really worried about their honour and reputation. This would make them think better of him, even though he's actually being really evil. Don John wants to see the trick through, even though it might get out of hand; "Grow this to what adverse issue it can, I will put it into practice." You could also mention how they both plot to stick to the same story so that the deception works.

Act 4, Scene 1 — You could write about how the friar realises that the best thing to do is to pretend that Hero really is dead, and to have a pretend funeral to "maintain a mourning ostentation". He says that this will make everyone feel sorry for her, when he says "lamented, pitied and excused". He claims that this will make everyone feel sorry for her even if she was guilty, and Claudio will realise what he's lost; "When he shall hear she died upon his words". You could also write about how she'll be remembered as a much better person than she actually was; "More moving-delicate and full of life". He thinks his plan is foolproof because "The supposition of the lady's death / Will quench the wonder of her infamy", so even if she is guilty, her death will distract people from the scandal.

3) To get all 18 marks you will need to comment on both scenes, and make about three points for each one. Remember to use quotes to back up your points.

Act 1, Scene 2 — You could write about how Ariel is very subservient towards Prospero because he wants to be granted his freedom. For example, he says "I will be correspondent to command" and calls Prospero a "noble master". He acts this way because he hopes to be granted his freedom if he works hard. You could write about how Caliban is very angry and bitter about his servitude to Prospero. When Prospero asks Caliban to fetch wood, Caliban retorts, "A south-west blow on ye / And blister you all o'er!". You could write about how Miranda and Prospero speak very roughly to Caliban and remind him constantly of his servitude, calling him a "poisonous slave" , "lying slave" and "Abhorred slave". They hate him because he tried to attack Miranda. You could write about how both Ariel and Caliban serve Prospero because of his powerful magic — neither of them have any choice. For example, Caliban says "I must obey. His art is of such power".

Act 5, Scene 1 — You could write about how Prospero bosses Ariel around because he is his slave, for example: "Ariel, / Fetch me the hat and rapier in my cell." You could write about how Prospero uses the prospect of freedom to motivate Ariel to carry out his orders: "Quickly, spirit / Thou shalt ere long be free." You could write about how Ariel is very happy at the thought of freedom, and sings as he does his work: "Merrily, merrily shall I live now".

Page 102 — Exam Questions

4) For 18 marks, cover both scenes and include a quotation or example to back up each point you make.
A good answer would make at least three points about each scene. Here are some suggestions:

Act 3, Scene 3 — You could write about Ariel's dramatic condemnation of Alonso, Antonio and Sebastian. He appears to them with "thunder and lightning" in the form of a mythical beast called a harpy and calls them "three men of sin". The intention is to frighten them and remind them of their guilt. Ariel claims that the storm and the loss of Ferdinand are retribution for their crimes against Prospero: "Thee of thy son, Alonso, / They have bereft". You could write about how Alonso is made to feel terribly guilty, believing that he has caused his son's death: "my son i' th' ooze is bedded. / I'll seek him deeper than e'er plummet sounded, / And with him there lie mudded." You could write about how Gonzalo observes the guilt of the other three men: "All three of them are desperate. Their great guilt, / Like poison given to work a great time after, / Now gins to bite the spirits".

Act 5, Scene 1 — You could write about how Prospero decides to forgive Alonso, Sebastian and Antonio. He forgives Antonio even though he has recently plotted to kill Alonso: "I do forgive thee, / Unnatural though thou art." You could write about how Alonso asks for forgiveness from Prospero for his crimes: "Thy dukedom I resign, and do entreat / Thou pardon me my wrongs". You could write about how Alonso's asking for forgiveness is rewarded. He is reunited with his son Ferdinand, whom he thought was dead: Sebastian says it's a "most high miracle!".

5) To get 18 marks for this question remember to write about both scenes.

Act 1, Scene 1 — You could write about how Richard pretends he doesn't know anything about Clarence being taken to the tower — "Upon what cause?" Mention how he blames the Queen; "the Queen's kindred are made gentlefolks". You could also write about his hypocrisy when he pretends to be upset: "this deep disgrace in brotherhood / Touches me deeper than you can imagine". He says he'll get Clarence freed, but then reveals that he's going to have Clarence killed; "tread the path that thou shalt ne'er return".

Act 3, Scene 7 — You could write about how Richard pretends to be praying, and to be doing what God wants "earnest in the service of my God". You could also mention how he claims he doesn't know why they've come to look for him. Write about how he's acting a part to make them believe that he doesn't really want to be King, when really that's exactly what he wants — "I would rather hide me from my greatness".

6) For the full 18 marks on this question you'll need to mention the curses and explain how and why Shakespeare makes future events seem inevitable, making about three good points for each scene.

Act 1, Scene 3 — Margaret speaks a lot in *asides* in this scene — Shakespeare shows the audience her true feelings. Margaret makes a prediction when she says that Richard will be King, but only of hell — "there thy kingdom is". She curses the young Prince Edward to "Die in his youth, by like untimely violence" — this comes true when the young princes are murdered in the tower. She curses Elizabeth that she will "live to wail thy children's death" and that she'll see someone else on the throne, which also comes true. She curses Rivers, Dorset and Hastings to an early and unnatural death: "none of you may live his natural age" and later in the play they are executed. She curses Richard too: "Thy friends suspect for traitors whilst thou liv'st,

/ And take deep traitors for thy dearest friends." This curse comes true as he has people loyal to him murdered, and is betrayed by Stanley. She also talks about "tormenting dream" which turns out to be true the night before the battle. However Buckingham is not directly cursed by Margaret; she warns him to beware of Richard: "take heed of yonder dog!" but he doesn't believe her.

Act 5, Scene 1 — You could write about how Buckingham feels that all the omens are being fulfilled when he walks to his execution, as he says "All-Soul's day is my body's doomsday" — he'd said that he'd vowed to die on that day if he betrayed King Edward and his family. He also refers directly to Margaret's curse, saying "Remember Margaret was a prophetess!"

Page 108 — Warm-up Questions

1) Two.
2) The shorter one will have a brief introduction to the topic, then some instructions on what to write. The longer one will probably give you a piece of text to read first — that will set the scene for the question.
3) **b** is the correct answer.
4) **b** is the correct answer. Keep to the point and choose your words carefully.
5) You might be asked to write an **article**, a **letter**, a **speech** or a **story**. There are several other forms they could ask for too.
6) You will get marks for a well organised and interesting writing style.
7) If the question says you "should" write about them then you must. Work your way through the list, covering every point.
8) a) Use the planning time to jot down some ideas in rough and then put them in order. It doesn't have to be neat.
   b) Yes. You won't get quite as long for the shorter question — about ten minutes — but it's still important to plan.
9) Use the last five minutes to go through your work and make it as accurate as you can. Check it for spellings and punctuation.

Page 113 — Warm-up Questions

1) False. You make a story interesting by planning exactly how to keep a reader hooked.
2) Yes. Make notes of what you want to include, then organise your notes into sections — even if you're not writing a story.
3) This is good advice.
4) a) This aims to persuade.
   b) This aims to inform.
   c) This aims to entertain.
5) **a, c** and **d** are correct.
6) Group 1 — your head teacher, your boss, your MP
   Group 2 — your penfriend, your mate, your grandma

Page 132 — Warm-up Questions

1) What actually happened that night was *horrifying*. I've never been so *panic-stricken* in my life. You'd have been *terrified* too if you'd been there. (*Terrified* and *panic-stricken* could be used the other way around.)
2) Work on choosing some effective verbs. Think about writing in sentences of different lengths too.
3) Sentences **b, c** and **e** would all impress an examiner. The other two are boring.
4) Use commas and full stops to break up the sentences. Try changing the word order in sentences too.
5) **b** is correct.
6) Get into the habit of looking up words you don't know in the dictionary as you come across them.
7) **a** would get higher marks. This version uses long and short sentences to build up tension.

Page 137 — Warm-up Questions

1) Include plenty of adjectives. Compare the things you are describing to something else.
2) They will tell you what things are like and help build up a picture.
3) The beginnings and endings should be matched up like this:
   He was as lazy as a toad at the bottom of a well.
   It made a sound like two trumpets and a sick donkey.
   She smiled like a crocodile with a good dentist.
   He wore a hat which looked like a beehive.
4) Sentences **a, d** and **e** have correct grammar.
5) They are not good comparisons because they don't make sense, e.g. bananas aren't pink. Better comparisons might be:
   a) He went as red as a tomato.

b) It was colder than an igloo.

c) Her voice was like nails scraping a blackboard.

6) **b** is correct. There's nothing wrong with exaggerating to make a point — just don't lie.
7) It is meant figuratively. His eyebrows weren't really caterpillars — they just looked like them.
8) False — it's OK to use the odd cliché, but if you use too many your writing will seem boring and unimaginative.

Page 143 — Warm-up Questions

1) **a** is an exaggeration that would be fair and effective in making your point. **b** is a lie and would lose you marks.
2) No — people will be put off if you sound too aggressive.
3) Yes — using personal words like 'we' makes the readers feel involved, and that they should be on the same side as you.
4) You might ask a question because the answer is obvious and you want to remind readers about that, e.g. "Do you want all our countryside to be gone by the time your children are born?"

   You might also ask a question to give yourself a chance to go on and write about the answer, e.g. "Why should we be concerned about junk food?"
5) Magic Threes are three adjectives next to each other, e.g. "fit, healthy and happy". They make descriptions sound more effective and convincing.

Page 145 — Exam Questions

1) For 30 marks you'll have to:

   • keep your tone formal, even though you'd probably be feeling fairly angry if this had happened in your school.
   • remember what head teachers might be worried about and what sort of things might persuade them.
   • deal with the problem incident first and then work your way towards finding a solution that will keep everyone happy.
   • plan your paragraphs — you get marks for paragraphs which link together well.

   This plan talks you through how you could answer this question:

   Keep your first paragraph short and explain why you're writing and what you hope to achieve. This sets the scene.

   You need to say why you're not happy. Your next paragraph could point out that only a few people are responsible for damaging classrooms and then ask if it's fair to punish the whole school. You'd need to keep it polite though and show you're on the same side. Say "I'm sure you will agree that the whole school doesn't deserve to be punished for the disgraceful actions of a few people" rather than "Do you honestly think it's fair to punish everybody even when it's not their fault?"

   It might be time for a bit of description next. Use your vocabulary and a few comparisons to build up a picture of how all the students are suffering from having to stay outside. You could mention how Year 9 can't get to the library to revise for their SATs perhaps. Make the head teacher feel sorry for all the decent, honest, hardworking students.

   In your next paragraph, start suggesting some solutions. One might be that each class could stick to their own form room and be responsible for keeping it tidy and ready for lessons in the afternoon. This would be the place to deal with any objections you think the head teacher might have to your ideas too.

   Examiners always look for a strong ending so don't just tail off. Finish with a "magic 3" perhaps. You could say "If we manage to agree on these proposals we will have a school that is a cheerful, comfortable and productive place for staff and students." You'll need a formal sign-off of some kind. "Thank you for taking the time to consider my ideas" would do, and then "Yours sincerely" if you've started with the head teacher's name. If you started with "Dear Sir" or "Dear Madam" it's "Yours faithfully".
2) To get the full 30 marks on this one, you need to:

   • cover a range of points which will appeal to a mixed audience of adults and children.
   • keep it fairly formal, as it's for an open evening.
   • plan so that you organise your speech into different sections before you begin to write it.
   • remember — you want them to change their travelling habits, so the things you mention have got to stay relevant to that.

   This plan talks you through how you could answer this question:

   You could start by explaining how so many people driving their children to school has become a problem. You might give examples of damage to health and high levels of pollution and describe the crowded roads in a way that makes them sound dangerous. Don't abuse the car-users — just politely point out that things are getting bad.

   In your middle section you could guess at what their objections might be to children travelling to school on foot or by bike, and then deal with them. For example, parents might feel that their children are at risk from strangers if they walk on their own. You could explain that if more children walked they would be in a group and therefore they would be safer.

   You need a strong finish for full marks and you want to end on a positive, encouraging note, so finish by describing the advantages to children and parents. Parents save time and money by not driving and their children develop independence and become fitter. For a dramatic finish, do a bit of comparing. Describe an unfit, unhealthy child who is driven everywhere and compare that to a healthy, capable child who walks. Then for your final question ask the parents which they'd rather have.

How to Mark The Practice Exam

Mark the Different Papers

Reading Paper

- Mark the **Reading** Questions just for reading comprehension. Don't knock off marks for badly written answers, or give more marks for well written ones.
- Add the scores up to get a mark out of **32**.

Writing Paper

- The Long Writing Question is marked for **sentence structure and punctuation**, **text structure and organisation** and **composition and effect**.
- The Short Writing Question is marked for **sentence structure, punctuation and text organisation**, **composition and effect** and **spelling**.
- Add up the separate marks to get a mark out of **50**.

Shakespeare Paper

- The Shakespeare question is only marked for **understanding** — there are no marks for the written style.
- You will get marks for **relevant points** which are backed up with **quotes** and **explanations**.
- It is worth **18** marks.

Work Out the **Level** from these Marks

1) Reading Score

Add the score out of 32 for the **Reading Paper** to the score out of 18 for the **Shakespeare Paper** to get a total **Reading Score** out of **50**, and look it up here:

TOTAL score out of 50	10 → 17	18 → 26	27 → 35	36 → 50
LEVEL	4	5	6	7

2) Writing Score

This is from your score out of 50 from the **Writing Paper**. Look up your level here:

TOTAL score out of 50	10 → 17	18 → 26	27 → 35	36 → 50
LEVEL	4	5	6	7

Important!

Getting Level 4, 5, 6 or 7 on one of these practice papers is **no guarantee** of getting that in the real SATs — **but** it's a pretty good guide.

3) Overall Level

To get an overall level, add together the **Reading** and **Writing** scores to get a mark out of **100**, then look it up here:

TOTAL score out of 100	20 → 34	35 → 52	53 → 70	71 → 100
LEVEL	4	5	6	7

Reading Paper Answers

1. 2 marks for any of the following quotations AND similar explanations, up to a maximum of 4 marks:

   • "David could feel himself bursting to be free" — shows it's uncomfortable in the classroom.

   • "The familiar classroom buzzed in the heat" — shows it's hot and busy in the classroom.

   • "the sun showed the chalk dust floating in front of the blackboard" — helps the reader to imagine how bright the sun is.

   • "his teacher moved slowly" — suggests everyone is too hot and bothered to move fast.

2. 1 mark for any of the following, up to a maximum of 2 marks:

   • David hopes he can still do times-tables championships.
   • He wants to hear a magical story on the carpet.
   • He collected frogspawn the week before.
   • He gets bored easily.

3. 1 mark for any of the following suggestions of things which show how David feels about Ben:

   he looks at Ben rather than another pupil / he remembers things Ben has done / he says Ben is the best in the class at not getting caught

   1 mark for any of the following explanations or similar:

   he admires him / they are friends / he wishes he could get away with things like Ben does / he likes the things he does

   Or other sensible, well explained ideas.

4. 2 marks for a good point with explanation, e.g.

   David doesn't want to leave the safety of the classroom he knows. I know this because it says, "He didn't want to move up."

   1 mark for a point without explanation, e.g.

   David feels sick of people saying the same things to him all the time about moving up.

5. 1 mark for any of the following ideas, up to a maximum of 3 marks.

   • David is not looking forward to leaving his current school. The story says "he didn't want to move up."

   • David is good at Maths, e.g. he often wins the times table championship.

   • David seems quite quiet and thoughtful — a lot of the story is about what he is thinking, he doesn't speak at all.

   • David is feeling under pressure to grow up and become a "young adult."

   • David is still quite childish — he enjoys things like listening to magical stories.

   Give a mark for other sensible, well thought out ideas.

6. bewilderment, terror
   [both answers needed for 1 mark]

7. 1 mark for any of the following, up to a maximum of 2 marks:

   • "I wept."

   • "It towered above me and all around me"

   • "It was knife-edged, dark, and a wicked green"

   • "I was lost"

   • "as though the sky was tearing apart."

   • "For the first time in my life I was out of the sight of humans."

   • "the sun hit me smartly on the face, like a bully."

8. 2 marks for a detailed impression, e.g.

   The impression I get of the cottage is that it is full of things to explore because it is set in a big garden and has a cellar. It doesn't seem very modern or comfortable because there are mushrooms on the ceiling.

   1 mark for a shorter answer, e.g.

   The cottage seems quite old and there are plants everywhere.

9. 1 mark for any of the following (or other reasonable answers), up to a maximum of 2 marks:

   • "Faces of rose, familiar, living"

   • "huge shining faces hung up like shields between me and the sky"

   • "faces with grins and white teeth (some broken) to be conjured up like genii with a howl"

   • "brushing off terror with their broad scoldings and affection"

10. ½ mark for any of the following or other reasonable answers, up to a maximum of 1 mark:

    • experts warned

    • doctors warned

    • heat exhaustion

    • highest factor suncream

11. 2 marks for an explanation mentioning that the scientists seem excited and confident, e.g.

    They seem to be excited about it because they're all competing to be the first to measure the highest temperature. They're described as "confident" that there will be a record set this week.

12. 2 marks for any of the following ideas (or other reasonable alternative) with explanation, up to a maximum of 4 marks:

    • A spokesperson for the Environment Agency has issued a statement — if an important body like this is getting involved the reader realises it is serious.

    • Reservoirs are almost dry — this is alarming and readers will start to wonder where they will get water from.

• Hosepipe bans — shows water is too scarce to waste

• Crops are failing — this could lead to problems with food production

• Minister for Education — is an important person so would only speak up if the situation was serious.

13. To gain full marks all bullet points must be addressed. Both texts must be written about. Full sentences must be used. Comparison words such as 'whereas' will help to gain marks. 1 mark for any of the following (or other reasonable points) up to a maximum of 5 marks:

The language the authors use:

• Both authors use lots of descriptive language, e.g. Laurie Lee describes himself as like a "fat young cuckoo", in 'Moving Up' the author describes how "the teacher moved slowly and heavily."

• Both texts use negative words like "bored" in 'Moving Up' and "nightmare" in 'Cider With Rosie'.

How you react to the texts:

• I think both the texts are good at showing the worries children experience about moving to a new place, whether it's a new home or a new school.

• I find it easier to believe in the character in 'Cider with Rosie' because it's written in the first person.

• I like the description of David's lesson in 'Moving Up' because I've been in lessons myself where it's really hot and I want to be outside.

Similarities and differences between the texts:

• 'Cider with Rosie' is an autobiography so it's based on real events, whereas 'Moving Up' is a fictional story.

• Both stories are set in the summer time and describe the heat, e.g. "the classroom buzzed in the heat", "honeyed tides of summer"

• David is older than Laurie Lee so his thoughts and experiences are different, e.g. Laurie Lee thinks about food and being lost, David thinks about school and friends.

• Both the authors describe the child's concerns, e.g. David worrying about moving schools, Laurie Lee worrying about being lost in the grass.

Writing Paper — Section A

Start by marking your long Writing answer for **composition and effect**.
Then mark it for **text structure and organisation** (page 182) and **sentence structure and punctuation** (page 183).
Add the marks you get for each one together to get your overall score out of **30**.

Composition and Effect

What's the Answer Like?	Mark
• Little understanding of audience and purpose of task. • Simple attempt to address content of task, for example, 'Welcome to this hotel.' • Basic information only, taken from question paper.	**0** marks
• Appropriate opening sentence that attempts to capture audience interest. • Some development of ideas about the hotel and what makes it attractive, for example, 'This hotel is the hotel of your dreams.' • Uses some descriptive and persuasive language, e.g. 'This lovely hotel is ideal for a good holiday.' • Uses an appropriate tone of voice in places.	**1-3** marks
• Style appropriate to audience and purpose. • Ideas developed more fully with more detail to persuade people to choose the hotel. • Varied vocabulary to sustain readers' interest. • Appropriate voice sustained, in places chatty and informal to target certain section of audience.	**4-6** marks
• Interesting and readable piece of writing, fully appropriate to audience and purpose. • Well organised content with developed descriptive vocabulary. • Makes use of stylistic devices such as rhetorical questions and humour. • Detailed development of ideas from question paper.	**7-9** marks
• Realistic text that is persuasive and interesting. • Audience and purpose fully targeted and readers' interest sustained. • Varied stylistic devices throughout writing to create impact and effect. • Detailed and fully developed points. • Varied tone of voice to target all members of audience.	**10-12** marks
• Imaginative and realistic writing, confidently sustained throughout piece. • Skilfully constructed and well organised writing that would persuade readers to go to the hotel. • Powerful descriptive language and persuasive devices. • Confident tone of voice, varying to take account of audience interest where appropriate.	**13-14** marks

Writing Paper — Section A continued

Text Structure and Organisation

WHAT'S THE ANSWER LIKE?	MARK
• Little structure, little attempt to open with an appropriate introductory sentence. • Little attempt to finish with an appropriate concluding sentence. • Few attempts at paragraphs or organisation of writing. • Some attempt to group together similar ideas.	**0** marks
• Attempts to open with a suitable introductory sentence, for example, "Welcome to this hotel". • Makes use of planning grid suggestions. • Ends with a suitable concluding sentence, for example, "It's a holiday not to be missed."	**1-2** marks
• Writing organised into sections or paragraphs. • Points and information developed with descriptive detail in places, for example, "The swimming pool is designed for fun, with big, colourful floats." • Simple connectives used to make piece of writing smooth and more interesting.	**3-4** marks
• Whole piece structured more clearly with link words or connectives used between paragraphs or sections, for example, "It's not just the pool that's great, the gym and sauna will appeal to everyone too." • Paragraphs or sections varied in structure, content and length to make piece more interesting. • Connectives used well within paragraphs or sections to link ideas and information.	**5-6** marks
• More complicated noun phrases used, for example, "If you loved the sound of the giant bedrooms with king-size beds, wait until you see the huge bar areas which are packed with oversize board games, pool tables and arcade games." • Paragraphs or sections well structured, easy to follow and persuasively signposted with appropriate phrases or words such as, "in addition", "as well", "not only". These phrases and words may be informal because of the nature of the task.	**7** marks
• Whole piece well structured, easy to follow, varied and interesting. • Content well organised for effect, for example to emphasise points, to draw readers' attention, to make things clearer. • Uses a range of devices, for example, bullet points, subheadings; as well as well-structured text. • Makes use of clear topic sentences to direct readers' attention.	**8** marks

Writing Paper — Section A

Sentence Structure and Punctuation

WHAT'S THE ANSWER LIKE?	MARK
• Uses only basic punctuation or no punctuation. • Simple noun phrases such as, "It is a good hotel." • Doesn't vary vocabulary, repeats subjects, connectives and simple verbs.	**0** marks
• Some sentences expanded with subordinate clauses. • Some variety in sentence structure. • Punctuation usually correct, but quite simple. • Mostly uses simple verbs, adverbs and adjectives.	**1-2** marks
• More connectives used, often simple but usually accurate. • Vocabulary a little more varied, including verbs. • More successful use of noun phrases and expanded noun phrases, such as, "This gorgeous, modern hotel has a lot of exciting themed bars to drink in." • Most punctuation accurate and some variety of punctuation used.	**3-4** marks
• Sentence length and structure more varied, for example, "This fantastic new hotel is full of all you'll need for that perfect holiday, whatever you're looking for. For a start, the beds are great." • Audience and purpose tackled with different sentence styles and types, for example, "Fancy a holiday you'll never forget? Let LastMinuteHotels sort you out." • Varied punctuation mostly used correctly and confidently. • Some varied vocabulary.	**5-6** marks
• Varied use of verbs, adverbs and adjectives. • Most clauses varied for effect, some expanded, some concise. • Punctuation varied for effect successfully, for example, dashes used to set conversational tone, rhetorical questions to draw in reader. • Confident variety of sentence lengths and styles.	**7** marks
• Successful and confident use of a variety of sentence styles, sustained throughout the piece for interest and effect. • Punctuation accurate, varied and sustained throughout the piece.	**8** marks

Writing Paper — Section B

Start by marking your short Writing answer for **sentence structure, punctuation and text organisation**. Next, mark the **spelling**. Then look at page 185 for info on how to mark it for **composition and effect**. Add the marks you get for each one together to get your overall score out of **20**.

Sentence Structure, Punctuation and Text Organisation

What's the Answer Like?	Mark
• Makes use of only very simple connectives, such as 'and'. • Makes no use of pronouns. • Most sentences constructed correctly, but basic. • Makes little or no use of punctuation beyond full stops and commas.	**0** marks
• Sometimes uses simple subordinate clauses to extend sentences. • Makes use of pronouns (e.g. he, she, it) • Beginning to use more complex sentences. • Sentences grouped together with the same topic. • More varied use of punctuation but still limited.	**1-2** marks
• Longer and more complex sentences, sometimes with several clauses. • Makes use of more complex verb forms, e.g. imperatives. • Sentences organised into paragraphs. • Points developed within paragraphs. • Punctuation used correctly and with some variety.	**3-4** marks
• Sustained use of complex sentences. • Sentence length and style varied for effect. • Range of connectives used effectively and confidently, both in sentences and between paragraphs. • Paragraphs clearly organised and flow smoothly. • Variety of punctuation used confidently and successfully.	**5** marks
• Able to use a range of verb forms consistently and successfully, including the passive voice to maintain an impersonal tone where appropriate. • Points clearly and thoroughly developed in detail. • Topic sentences used to begin paragraphs, paragraphs organised carefully for maximum effect. • Confident use of varied punctuation to good effect.	**6** marks

Spelling

What's the Answer Like?	Mark
• Simple words of one syllable are spelt correctly. • Common words of more than one syllable are spelt correctly, e.g. 'because'. • Some words are confused with each other, e.g. here / hear. • Some words are spelt as they sound, e.g. 'secondry'.	**1** mark
• Most words that follow a regular pattern are spelt correctly. • Some more difficult words are spelt incorrectly, e.g. recieve. • Some prefixes and suffixes are spelt incorrectly, e.g. dissappeared.	**2** marks
• Most words are spelt correctly, including unusual words. • Some minor mistakes are made, e.g. unstressed vowels are missed out. • There are occasional mistakes with more difficult words.	**3** marks
• Almost every word spelt perfectly. • Any very minor slips are rare and not repeated.	**4** marks

Writing Paper — Section B

Composition and Effect

What's the Answer Like?	Mark
• Little awareness of task, or the audience and purpose of the task. • Little detail, brief piece of writing.	**0** marks
• Some awareness of audience and purpose. • Opening sentence appropriate to the style of a newspaper report, for example, 'Claims have been made about ghosts living in Clumby Castle…' • Impersonal tone sometimes used where appropriate, for example to give information about the haunted castle. • Some unevenness in tone and style.	**1-3** marks
• Good awareness of audience and purpose. • Detailed and developed writing, in an appropriate informal tone, usually sustained. • Style and tone capture and maintain audience interest using, for example, humour, anecdote, rhetorical questions.	**4-6** marks
• Makes use of descriptive details and devices, for example, "It wasn't until we all felt the temperature drop that we realised something sinister was going on. The whole group felt uneasy and there was a lot of anxiety in the air." • Confident style and tone appropriate to audience and purpose. • Good mix of impersonal tone for reporting information, and a more personal voice for description or anecdote. • Good variety of stylistic devices to sustain readers' interest.	**7-9** marks
• Confident and convincing piece of writing. • Effective description and interesting style throughout. • Imaginative writing with fully developed ideas.	**10** marks

Shakespeare Paper Answers

1) Count up the number of separate points made to answer the question in the essay. On the grid below, tick one box for each point (up to 6 ticks).
2) Tick one box for every one of those points that's backed up by a quote (up to 6 ticks).
3) Then tick one box for every point that's expanded with a comment (up to 6 ticks).
4) Finally count up all the ticks to give a mark out of **18**.

Shakespeare Paper

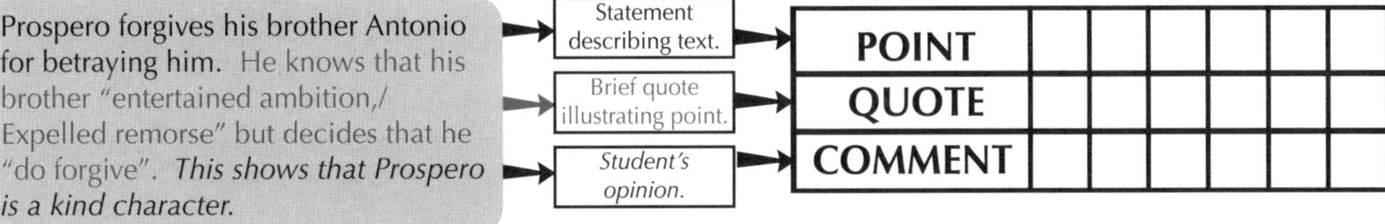

If you want to be really ready for the exam, you need to do more practice papers.
You can either hassle your teacher for past papers, or buy CGP's pack of specially written practice papers.
Up to you.

Index

Index

Make sure you're not missing out on another superb CGP revision book that might just save your life...

...order your **free** catalogue today.

CGP customer service is second to none

We work very hard to despatch all orders the **same day** we receive them, and our success rate is currently 99.9%. We send all orders by **overnight courier** or **First Class** post.
If you ring us today you should get your catalogue or book tomorrow. Irresistible, surely?

- Phone: 0870 750 1252 (Mon-Fri, 8.30am to 5.30pm)
- Fax: 0870 750 1292
- e-mail: orders@cgpbooks.co.uk
- Post: CGP, Kirkby-in-Furness, Cumbria, LA17 7WZ
- Website: www.cgpbooks.co.uk

...or you can ask at any good bookshop.

EHS31